A
Civil War
Doctor

TITLES IN THE WORKING LIFE SERIES INCLUDE:

An Actor on the Elizabethan Stage

The Cavalry During the Civil War

A Colonial Craftsman

A Medieval Knight

A Medieval Merchant

A Medieval Monk

A Mountain Man on the American Frontier

A Renaissance Painter

A Roman Gladiator

A Roman Senator

A Sweatshop During the Industrial Revolution

A Worker on the Transcontinental Railroad

THE WORKING LIFE

A Civil War Doctor

MICHAEL V. USCHAN

LUCENT BOOKS

An imprint of Thomson Gale, a part of The Thomson Corporation

Detroit • New York • San Francisco • San Diego • New Haven, Conn.
Waterville, Maine • London • Munich

To Dr. Daniel Donovan, a physician who
treats the people he cares for as human
beings and not simply as patients.

LIBRARY OF CONGRESS CATALOGING-IN-PUBLICATION DATA

Uschan, Michael V., 1948–
  A Civil War doctor / by Michael Uschan.
    p. cm. — (The working life series)
  Includes bibliographical references and index.
  ISBN 1-59018-578-1 (hard cover : alk. paper)
  1. United States—History—Civil War, 1861–1865—Medical care—Juvenile literature. 2. Physicians—United States—History—19th century—Juvenile literature. 3. Surgeons—United States—History—19th century—Juvenile literature. 4. Medicine, Military—United States—History—19th century—Juvenile literature. I. Title. II. Series.
E621.U83 2005
973.7'75'0922—dc22

2004027101

Printed in the United States of America

CONTENTS

FOREWORD

"The strongest bond of human sympathy outside the family relations should be one uniting all working people of all nations and tongues and kindreds."

Abraham Lincoln, 1864

Work is a common activity in which almost all people engage. It is probably the most universal of human experiences. As Henry Ford, inventor of the Model T, said, "There will never be a system invented which will do away with the necessity of work." For many people, work takes up most of their day. They spend more time with their coworkers than with family and friends. And the common goals people pursue on the job may be among the first thoughts that they have in the morning, and the last that they may have at night.

While the idea of work is universal, the way it is done and who performs it vary considerably throughout history. The story of work is inextricably tied to the history of technology, the history of culture, and the history of gender and race. When the typewriter was invented, for example, it was considered the exclusive domain of men who worked as secretaries. As women workers became more accepted, the secretarial role was gradually filled by women. Finally, with the invention of the computer, the modern secretary spends little time actually typing correspondence. Files are delivered via computer, and more time is spent on other tasks than the manual typing of correspondence and business.

This is just one example of how work brings together technology, gender, and culture. Another example is the American plantation slave. The harvesting of cotton was initially so cumbersome and time consuming that even with slaves its profitability was doubtful. With the invention of the cotton gin, however, efficiency improved, and slavery became a viable agricultural tool. It also became a Southern tradition and institution, enough that the South was willing to go to war to preserve it.

The books in Lucent's Working Life series strive to show the intermingling of work, and its reflection in culture, technology, race, and gen-

6

der. Indeed, history viewed through the perspective of the average worker is both enlightening and fascinating. Take the history of the typewriter, mentioned above. Readers today have access to more technology than any of their historical counterparts, and, in fact, though they would find the typewriter's keyboard familiar, they would find using it a bore. Finding out that people spent their days sitting over that machine (with no talk of carpal tunnel syndrome!) and were valued if they made no typing errors because corrections were cumbersome to make and, in some legal professions, made documents invalid, is an interesting story that involves many different aspects of history.

The desire to work is almost innate. As German socialist Ferdinand Lassalle said in the 1850s, "Workingmen we all are so far as we have the desire to make ourselves useful to human society in any way whatever." Yet each historical period offers a million different stories of the history of each job and how it was performed. And that history is the history of human society.

Each book in the Working Life series strives to tell the tale of these anonymous workers. Primary source quotes offer veracity and immediacy to each volume, letting the workers themselves tell their stories. In addition, thorough bibliographies tell students where they can find out more information, and complete indexes allow for easy perusal of the text. While students learn about the work of years gone by, they gain empathy for those who toil and, perhaps, a universal pride in taking up the work that will someday be theirs.

WHY DOCTORS
WENT TO WAR

The Civil War was the most terrible war in American history, a bloody conflict that almost divided the United States of America forever. It began at 4:30 A.M. on April 12, 1861, when soldiers for the newly formed Confederate States of America began firing cannons at Fort Sumter, a U.S. military facility on a small island in the Charleston, South Carolina, harbor.

The booming shots that ignited war climaxed decades of political strife over the intertwined issues of slavery and states' rights. Northerners believed slavery should be abolished and that the federal government had the

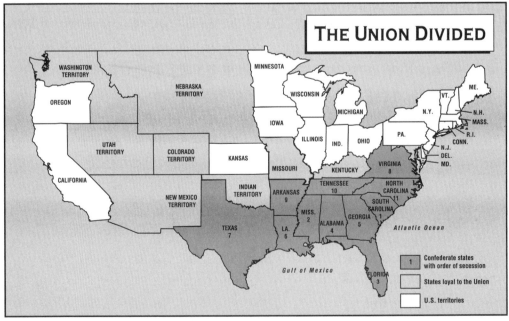

THE UNION DIVIDED

Confederate states with order of secession

States loyal to the Union

U.S. territories

power to do so. Southerners, however, believed they needed the cheap labor that slaves provided to power the South's agricultural economy, which included vast cotton plantations tended by hundreds of slaves. Southerners also believed that individual states alone had the authority to abolish or preserve slavery, which most Southern state governments favored and wanted to continue.

On November 6, 1860, when Abraham Lincoln was elected president, this divisiveness erupted into the worst political crisis in U.S. history. Lincoln, who was slavery's most eloquent opponent, had run on a Republican Party platform that claimed it was immoral to own other people. Fearing that Lincoln would try to outlaw the practice throughout America, many Southern states decided to leave the United States and form their own nation to ensure that their residents could continue to own slaves.

On December 20 South Carolina became the first of thirteen Southern states to secede from the Union and join the new Confederate States of America. The line between proslavery and antislavery states was drawn, and with the nation split in half, civil war was inevitable.

WHAT MOTIVATED DOCTORS

When the cannons roared at Fort Sumter, doctors on both sides of the conflict volunteered to serve. The main reason most of them decided to go to war was the slavery issue. Benjamin Woodward, a surgeon for the Twenty-second Regiment of the Illinois Infantry Volunteers, was among many Union doctors who believed slavery was immoral and had to be ended. On November 10, 1861, Woodward explained how strongly he and other Northern soldiers felt about slavery when he responded to a letter from his wife. Woodward wrote: "In one of your letters you said that it had been reported in Galesburg [Illinois] that the army was not in favor of liberating the slaves. All I can say is that I have talked with many thousands on the subject, and have heard but one wish . . . that the war will not terminate till slavery is put down."[1]

Some Confederate doctors were as passionate about supporting slavery as Woodward and his colleagues were in opposing it. Several physicians thought the South needed slavery to survive economically, and others backed the war because they believed the U.S. government did not have the legal right to force individual states to ban slavery or accede to any other demand. Joseph Le Conte, a South Carolina doctor who helped manufacture medical drugs for the Confederacy, was among the latter group. In his autobiography, Le Conte claimed the war was really about how the nation should be governed: "It was an honest difference of

Union surgeons prepare to amputate a wounded soldier's leg. The doctor on the right holds the patient's limb while another in the center holds a knife and a third (left) holds a saw.

opinion as to the nature of our government; it was honestly fought out to a finish and the result frankly accepted. To us it was literally a life and death struggle for national existence; and doubtless the feeling was equally honest and earnest on the other side."[2]

Union and Confederate doctors and other soldiers, however, also went to war for other reasons. Many Northerners fought because they were angry Southern states had divided America; they wanted to defeat the Confederacy and reunite the nation. Some Southerners went to war because they were angry the North would not let them have their own nation and

because Union soldiers invaded their homeland after Fort Sumter to force them to return to the Union.

But many doctors on both sides had a more personal motivation for fighting, one that had nothing to do with slavery or patriotic feelings toward their respective nations. Many physicians went to war for the opportunity to improve their medical skills by learning about battle wounds and illnesses they might never otherwise encounter. Union surgeon Edward L. Munson explains:

[Physicians] flocked to the colors [joined their respective armies] almost en masse, not only from motives of patriotism, but also because the [medical] training to be gained in the vast military [effort] was far more comprehensive and valuable than could be gained in any similar civil[ian] institute or walk of life.[3]

ALL THE WORK THEY WANTED

Doctors got more opportunities to learn than they could ever have imagined. In the four years the Civil War lasted, it is estimated that Union and Confederate physicians treated more than a half million soldiers with combat wounds and more than 9 million soldiers with diseases such as diarrhea, measles, smallpox, and typhoid fever. By dealing with so many wounded and sick soldiers, doctors learned a great deal. As one Confederate surgeon wrote after the war, "I have lost much, but I have gained much, especially as a medical man. I return home a better surgeon, a better doctor."[4] Those physicians also saved the lives of tens of thousands of Union and Confederate soldiers who would have died without their care.

CHAPTER 1

A WAR FOR WHICH DOCTORS WERE ILL-PREPARED

Even though the Civil War had long been expected prior to 1861, neither the Union nor the Confederacy was prepared for the immense scale of the terrible conflict, which engulfed the nation over the next four years. And perhaps no branch of the military was less ready to handle the consequences of war than the surgeons—the military term for doctors—who would care for millions of sick and wounded soldiers. Union surgeon Richard Swanton Vickery acknowledged that the tremendous tasks confronting doctors initially overwhelmed them:

This war, unprecedented in modern times for the numbers of men engaged on both sides, the fearful slaughter of its numerous battlefields and the consequent number of wounded requiring the Surgeon's care, found the Medical Department, like the other Departments of the army, not prepared for demands [placed] upon it on such an enlarged scale.[5]

The main problem both sides had in gearing up for war was that it was the largest conflict in which Americans had ever fought. Prior to the conflict, the U.S. Army had only 15,000 soldiers. But in the fighting that continued from Fort Sumter on April 12, 1861, until the South surrendered on April 9, 1865, nearly 3 million Union soldiers battled 1.5 million Confederates. The conflict's immense size is evident in the 620,000 soldiers who died—360,000 on the Union side and 260,000 for the Confederacy—a total greater than the number of Americans killed in all other wars combined, from the American Revolution until the Vietnam War.

This toll would have been much higher without the Union and

The corpses of Union soldiers litter the battlefield at Gettysburg, Pennsylvania, in July 1863. The three-day battle resulted in nearly 8,000 deaths, and almost 27,000 more soldiers were wounded.

Confederate medical departments, the military organizations in which doctors performed their work. Recruiting thousands of doctors for them was one of the most difficult tasks both sides faced.

DESPERATE FOR DOCTORS

Although the Union used more than 12,000 doctors and the Confederacy more than 3,000, when the fighting began neither side had more than a handful of physicians. In 1860 the Union had 114 doctors, but 24 resigned to fight for the Confederacy and 3 others were dismissed for disloyalty because they favored the Southern cause. The Union doctors who resigned became the nucleus of the fledgling Confederate Medical Department.

Both sides were so desperate to recruit physicians that they accepted anyone claiming to be a doctor.

Because there were no universally recognized professional standards for doctors at the time, both armies enlisted many people with little or no medical knowledge or skill. Complaining about a poorly trained physician he worked with at Chesapeake Hospital in Virginia, Union surgeon David Warman wrote in his diary, "Dr. Crombie was only a country practitioner and had never written a prescription [for medicine] in his life. I had to instruct him how to do it. We had too many of these country practitioners in the Army during the War."[6]

When incompetent physicians treated ill or wounded soldiers, the patients rarely got better, and some died from such poor care. By the end of 1861, some doctors had performed so badly that Confederate secretary of war Judah P. Benjamin admitted, "Quite a number who had been appointed have proven unequal to the duties of their station [and] in some instances there was gross ignorance of the very elements of the profession."[7] Decades after the war ended, Edward L. Munson admitted that the Union was also not careful in selecting physicians:

The ablest as well as the most ignorant [medical] practitioners in the land were eligible for appointment. Such as came into the army without receiving a [medical school] diploma were permitted to experiment with the lives and health of their patients, until found incompetent they were brought before a [review] board and dismissed from service.[8]

In 1862 both sides began ridding their ranks of poorly trained doctors and making future applicants pass a test on medical knowledge. The examinations lasted several days and included questions about anatomy, medical theories, and how to treat patients for various illnesses. The tests were so demanding that many applicants could not pass them. When George E. Waller failed the Confederate exam, he wrote to his family, "I was not at all disappointed when I was pitched [not accepted] for I had talked with [a doctor] prior to my examination and he told me that four out of five were thrown [failed]."[9]

Those who passed were well-educated physicians. However, the era's medical knowledge was so primitive that even those accepted by the military were ill-prepared to deal with the war's terrible physical injuries and illnesses.

"MEDICAL MIDDLE AGES"

Most of the younger doctors in both armies had attended one of the nation's more than forty medical schools, most of which were in Northern states. Prewar medical study consisted of a series of lectures about medical knowledge spread over nine months. The same lectures were repeated the following year to conclude a doctor's education. Many older doctors, however, never attended medical school. Instead, they learned by studying with established physicians. The quality of the education they gained in this apprenticeship depended on how much the doctor knew and how well he could teach his student.

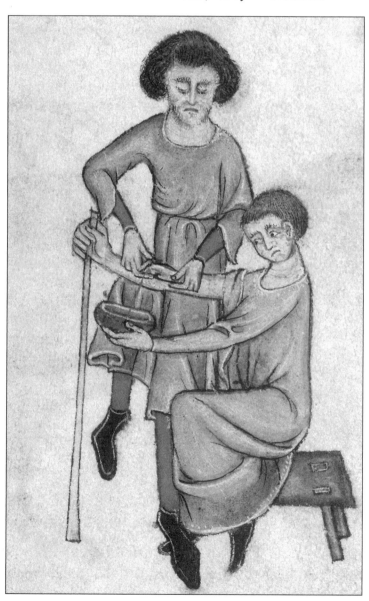

A fourteenth-century image depicts a European physician bleeding a patient. Such practices were still used five hundred years later during the American Civil War.

Even the era's most advanced medical knowledge was primitive compared to what doctors learn today. William A. Hammond, surgeon general of the Union Medical Department, claimed decades later that when the war began medical knowledge was only just approaching "the end of the medical Middle Ages."[10] The Middle Ages was a historical period in Europe marked by widespread ignorance and a lack of education. Hammond compared the state of Civil War medicine to that era to stress the inferior knowledge doctors had.

The most glaring defect in medical knowledge was that doctors did not know what caused disease. They believed illnesses such as diarrhea, typhoid fever, and measles were due to "miasms," pockets of bad air produced by nature. In fact, the name of one of the period's most deadly diseases—malaria—comes from the Latin words *mala* ("bad") and *aria* ("air"). In 1862, when measles and typhoid fever sickened thousands of soldiers in Virginia, Union surgeon J.J. Allen simply argued, "This region is proverbial for almost every variety of miasmatic fever."[11]

This spring lancet was a tool commonly used by Civil War doctors to open a patient's vein and release the illness in the blood that had been caused by bad air.

Ignorance about what caused disease led doctors to treat their patients in ways that seem bizarre today. The most common treatment was bleeding, in which doctors made cuts in the patient's skin to drain blood and thus rid the body of illness produced by miasms. A variation of this method was cupping, in which a warmed glass was placed over a cut in the skin; when the glass cooled, it created a vacuum that sucked out blood and illness. Similarly, in blistering, hot plasters were placed on the skin to form blisters, which were then drained to remove disease.

Their lack of knowledge about disease and how the body worked limited doctors in the surgery they could perform. Because physicians did not understand how the heart and other organs functioned or the diseases that affected them, they rarely operated inside the chest or abdominal cavity. Surgery was mainly limited to cleaning open wounds, setting broken bones, and amputating badly injured fingers, arms, and legs. Because of this, soldiers with abdominal, chest, and head injuries often died because doctors did not know how to treat their wounds.

The medical "Middle Ages" that Hammond referred to ended in the decades following the war because of scientific discoveries. The most important new medical knowledge was that bacteria and viruses, which are living

organisms, cause diseases like typhoid fever and diarrhea as well as infections in wounds. This knowledge could have saved many lives because disease and infection killed twice as many soldiers as battle wounds during the war. In 1906 Confederate assistant surgeon William H. Taylor commented in a speech on the inferior knowledge doctors had. "As to our methods," said Taylor, "I may say, as a general statement, that we aimed to conform to the science of the time [but] what we knew of military medicine, compared with what is known of it now, seems small and of inferior quality."[12]

INEXPERIENCED DOCTORS

In addition to going to war armed with medical knowledge that was flawed by modern standards, only a handful of physicians on either side had ever treated gunshot wounds or other injuries associated with warfare. This inexperience left them unprepared to deal with the horrific injuries combat produced. Confederate surgeon Herbert M. Nash noted, "The surgical staff of the army was composed of general practitioners from all parts of the Southern country whose previous professional life, during the period of unbroken peace which preceded the Civil War, gave them but little surgery and very seldom presented a gunshot wound."[13]

Even the few doctors who had served in the military found themselves

Wounded men lie on the battlefield in Spotsylvania, Virginia, in May 1864. A significant percentage of wounded Civil War soldiers did not survive their medical treatment.

confronted by new medical challenges brought about by advancements in weapons. The rifles most soldiers carried had barrels with spiral grooves, a technological innovation that enabled them to shoot greater distances and with more power and accuracy than old-fashioned muskets with smooth barrels. These rifles also fired a new bullet—the minié ball. Made of soft lead, the minié ball expanded on impact to tear huge holes in the target's body and shatter any bones that it struck. Recognizing that such devastating new types of wounds made it more difficult for doctors to save lives, Confederate assistant surgeon Taylor commented, "From the standpoint of the army surgeon, the horrors of war have been vastly augmented by modern advances."[14]

Because so many doctors were young men, often recent medical school graduates, they were also inexperienced in treating patients for any type of injury or illness. For example, Simon Baruch went straight from college to the Confederate army. After the war, Baruch admitted how poorly prepared he had been to function as a military surgeon:

The great need of army surgeons may be understood by you when

I tell you that before ever treating a sick person or even having lanced a boil and still under the age of 22 I was appointed assistant surgeon and placed in charge of [caring for] 500 infantry [soldiers], with only a hospital steward [aide] to assist me.[15]

Veteran doctors like Union surgeon Benjamin Woodward, however, were usually not much more experienced than youngsters like Baruch when it came to surgery. After a battle on October 9, 1861, Woodward wrote to his wife that he was amazed at how many operations he had done. He stated, "I have seen more surgery than I could in 50 years private practice."[16] In fact, only five hundred Union doctors and twenty-seven Confederate physicians had performed any type of surgery before the war. They all had to learn how to perform a variety of operations, from removing bullets to amputating limbs. After the First

❧ A YOUNG DOCTOR GOES TO WAR ❧

Some doctors served as Civil War surgeons before they finished medical school. One was W.W. Keen, who, in 1861, interrupted his medical studies at Jefferson Medical College in Philadelphia to become an assistant surgeon. Keen worked as a Union doctor for four months before returning to school to finish his studies. In 1862 he resumed his military duties. The story of how Keen was plucked from college to go to war is from his memoir, which has been reproduced on the Web site of the Society of Civil War Surgeons:

I had the honor of being sworn into the service of the United States as an assistant surgeon in the shadow of the Capitol [in Washington, D.C.,] on July 4, 1861, though I had only begun the study of medicine in September, 1860, and did not graduate until March, 1862.

It came about in this [way]: My [faculty adviser], Dr. John H. Brinton, had received a telegram from a former student (let us call him Smith) who had graduated in March, 1861, and was assistant surgeon of the Fifth Massachusetts, saying that he was going to leave the regiment and asking that Dr. Brinton should immediately send some one in his place, if possible. Dr. Brinton very kindly offered the place to me. I said to him, with very becoming modesty, that I hardly felt I knew enough; to which he replied, with combined frankness and flattery, by saying: "It is perfectly true that you know very little, but, on the other hand, you know a good deal more than Smith." Accordingly I entered the army and immediately went into camp in Alexandria [Virginia].

❧ CONFEDERATE SICK CALL ☙

One of a Civil War doctor's most important daily duties was sick call. At a set time every morning, ill soldiers reported to their unit's doctor for medical care. The primitive nature of health care during this period can be seen from the way Confederate assistant surgeon William H. Taylor handled sick call. Taylor's explanation of his medical routine is from Doctors in Gray: The Confederate Medical Service *by H.H. Cunningham.*

Early in the morning we had sick-call, when those who claimed to be ill or disabled came up to be [examined]. Diagnosis was rapidly made, usually by intuition [looking at the soldier], and treatment was with such drugs as we chanced to have in the knap-sack [which an aide carried] and were handiest to obtain. In serious cases we made an honest effort to bring to bear all the skill and knowledge we possessed, but our science could rarely display itself to the best advantage on account of the paucity of our resources. On the march my own practice was of necessity still further simplified, and was, in fact, reduced to the lowest terms. In one pocket of my trousers I had a ball of blue mass [mercury mixed with chalk], in another a ball of opium. All complainants were asked the same question, "How are your bowels?" If they were open, I administered a plug of opium; if they were shut, I gave a plug of blue mass.

Battle of Bull Run in July 1861, Confederate E.A. Craighill commented on this lack of knowledge: "There were surgeons in our army older than I was, who had much more experience, but none of us up to that time had seen much of gunshot wounds, and we had to unlearn what we had been taught at college, in books [because] only experience was useful in treatment."[17]

MILITARY SURGEONS

Craighill and other doctors found that tending wounds in real life was far different from the way they had been taught by textbooks. In addition to learning how to treat new injuries, doctors also had to accustom themselves to military life.

Doctors in the Union and Confederate armies were called either a surgeon or an assistant surgeon; the latter designation was for less-experienced doctors. Although military records for both sides usually refer to them by those titles, physicians also had a military rank. A surgeon was usually made a major or a captain, whereas an assistant surgeon commonly became a captain or a lieutenant. During the war the Union commissioned 2,109 surgeons and 3,882 assistant surgeons; the Confederacy, meanwhile, appointed 1,242 surgeons and 1,994 assistant surgeons. Each regiment, the basic military unit of about one thousand soldiers, had at least 1 surgeon and 1 assistant surgeon. There were additional doctors for each brigade, which was composed of three to four regiments.

Many doctors at first had trouble doing their jobs because they had never served in the military. They had to become familiar with military customs, such as how to salute superior officers, and learn to handle new duties like sick call, the time each day when ill soldiers reported to be examined. Union surgeon Charles S. Tripler, medical director of the Army of the Potomac, commented on problems doctors had in adjusting to military life when the Civil War began. He acknowledged, "For the most part, physicians taken suddenly from civil[ian] life, with little knowledge of their [military] duties, had to be taught them from the very alphabet [the basics]. Hence confusion, conflict of interest, and discontent very seriously impaired efficiency in the medical department."[18]

Many doctors had trouble learning to cope with regulations and the rigid military command structure. This problem was even more severe for thousands of civilian doctors who at times cared for soldiers.

CONTRACT SURGEONS

After every major battle, local doctors volunteered to help tend wounded soldiers. They did this because there were usually more wounded than military doctors could quickly treat; their help was appreciated because they saved many lives. Both sides also hired contract surgeons, doctors who signed contracts to work for a specified period of time. The length of their contracts varied from weeks to years depending on the duties they were hired to perform.

Although some contract surgeons worked at the scenes of major battles, most were placed in hospitals far from the fighting. This was done because their ignorance of the military created problems when they worked with army units. For example, in 1864 Contract Surgeon David Warman was employed at Chesapeake Hospital in Virginia. After visiting Fort Monroe, Warman had a heated argument with a guard because he did not know he needed a military password to leave the heavily guarded facility, which housed some Confederate prisoners of war. Warman recorded in his diary, "I was about to leave the Fort at the outer gate when a sentinel shouted, 'Who goes there?' and pointed a bayonet to my breast and demanded the countersign [password]. Then I had to go back to officers in command and get the countersign before I was let outside the stone walls of the Fortress."[19]

The Union employed fifty-five hundred contract surgeons during the war. Because most Confederate records were destroyed, it is not known how many contract surgeons the South hired. Although both sides needed them, military doctors looked down on their civilian counterparts. The dislike was partly due to jealousy that contract surgeons were paid more—one hundred dollars a month—but also because the army doctors considered civilians useless in battle. Dr. Jonathan Letterman, medical director of the Army of the Potomac beginning in June 1862, harshly criticized civilian doctors in his report on the Battle of Gettysburg. He wrote, "No reliance can be placed on surgeons from civil[ian] life during or after a battle. [The] great majority think more of their own [personal] comfort than they do of the wounded."[20]

Military doctors also tended to resent civilian doctors because many seemed to care only about honing their surgical skills. While serving on the *City of Memphis*, a hospital ship carrying soldiers wounded from the Battle of Shiloh, Union surgeon N.R. Derby claimed some doctors were so eager to do this that they performed unnecessary operations. In his diary entry for April 7, 1862, Derby wrote,

Many [doctors] doing duty on the hospital steamer during those days were volunteers, and, as they had come down to operate, and were greatly desirous of doing so, I found it necessary to dedicate some portion of my time to the preservation of limbs that were about to be unnecessarily placed under the knife.[21]

MEDICAL CADETS

A third group of medical officers was especially eager to learn. Those were medical cadets, students who had not yet finished medical school but knew enough to ably assist doctors.

The scarcity of physicians led the Union in 1861 to enlist medical students as young as eighteen. The Confederates, whose need was even more desperate, also used students. Although no more than seventy were allowed in the Union army at one time, almost three hundred served during the war. For cadets, it was a wonderful opportunity to gain medical experience and knowledge. In July 1862 Cadet Edwin Hutchinson wrote exaltedly to his mother about how much he could learn: "I will probably see more patients and have a chance to give more medicine [in a few months] than I could in two years of practice. I could not possibly have a better opportunity for acquiring knowledge of medicine than that I now enjoy."[22]

Although most cadets worked in large hospitals under the supervision

❧ THE SONG OF THE MEDICAL CADETS ❧

One of the Civil War's most famous medical cadets was Edward Curtis. Like many medical students who served as cadets, Curtis later became a Union surgeon. He is noted in history for being one of the doctors who helped examine the body of President Abraham Lincoln after he was assassinated.

While working as a cadet at West Philadelphia General Hospital, Curtis wrote a song about the experiences of medical cadets that was a parody of a popular song of the time called "Gay and Happy." The lyrics of his song, printed here, are taken from a story on medical cadets in the Journal of the American College of Surgeons:

THE MEDICAL CADETS HYMN

We're the Med. Cads. gay and happy
Summoned from our homes to save
By the Surgeon's holy mission
Wounded warriors from the grave.

Chorus:
So let the war be waged as it will
We'll be gay & happy still
Gay & happy, gay & happy
We'll be gay & happy still.

Falls a soldier in the battle
Stricken by a Rebel ball
We, the Med. Cads. kneel beside him
Mindful then of duty's call.
Chorus [repeat]

Ours the art to soothe the anguish
Of each ragged gaping wound
Tending every stricken warrior
Thickly as they strew the ground.
Chorus [repeat]

Loud may roar the war around us
Nought care we for shot or shell
Pledged we stand to save the fallen
Though we face the fires of hell.
Chorus [repeat]

Edward Curtis was a medical cadet who graduated to become a Union surgeon during the war.

of doctors, some were assigned to battle zones. Their duties generally involved routine chores like changing bandages, but some talented cadets were given more complex responsibilities, and a few performed surgery. Many cadets returned to medical school after their one-year enlistment to finish their studies. When they graduated, more than one hundred returned to the Union army as surgeons.

BETTER DOCTORS

Although inexperience hampered doctors when the conflict began, bloody battles like Antietam, Bull Run, Gettysburg, and Shiloh became dramatic classrooms in which they learned how to save lives. Hunter Holmes McGuire, one of the Confederacy's ablest doctors, once commented on

how quickly untested doctors became able military surgeons. Claimed McGuire:

> Coming from civil[ian] life, it was wonderful to see how rapidly [a doctor] adapted himself to the discipline of the army and conformed to the requirements of military life. The hardships he endured and the privations to which he was subjected soon transformed him from a novice to a veteran, and I can say, with truth, that before the war ended some of the best military surgeons in the world could be found in the Confederate army.[23]

Union surgeons learned the same hard lessons while toiling on the opposite side in the Civil War.

CHAPTER 2

TREATING SOLDIERS WOUNDED IN BATTLE

The most important and difficult job Civil War doctors had was caring for soldiers wounded in battle. On September 19, 1862, when more than seven thousand soldiers clashed in the Battle of Iuka in Mississippi, the two sides suffered nearly fifteen hundred casualties, a military term that includes soldiers killed, wounded, or missing in action. Surgeon A.B. Campbell, medical director of the Army of the Mississippi, issued a glowing report about how swiftly and efficiently seven hundred Confederate doctors treated casualties:

> The battle was fought so close to the hospital that the men detailed as bearers [of wounded] could go to the [battle] and return at short intervals. The moment a man fell he was taken up, and in three minutes his wounds were being dressed. All necessary operations

were performed at once, and the records show but a trifling mortality [deaths].[24]

In most of the war's battles, however, it was much harder to perform this vital task, especially in conflicts involving large numbers of soldiers. For example, on August 29–30, 1862, the Confederates soundly defeated the Union in the Second Battle of Bull Run in Virginia. One week after the fighting had ended, Union surgeon general William A. Hammond reported on long delays in treating sixteen thousand wounded soldiers. On September 7, Hammond wrote:

> Up to this date, 600 wounded still remain on the battlefield, in consequence of an insufficiency of ambulances and the want of a proper system of regulating their removal. Many have died

of starvation; many more will die in consequence of exhaustion, and all have endured torments which might have been avoided.[25]

The difference in the two battles was how quickly soldiers received medical attention. Speed was important because any delay in care resulted in more deaths due to loss of blood, shock, or infection. Because of this, transporting soldiers and treating them as quickly as possible became a vital part of Civil War medical care.

DR. LETTERMAN'S PLAN

When the war began, neither side had adequate plans on how to quickly evacuate wounded soldiers from battlefields and speedily treat them. Surgeon Jonathan Letterman, medical director of the Army of the Potomac, explains why combat made this difficult:

On the field of battle confusion is, above all other places, most prone to ensue, and unless some method is observed by which certain surgeons have specific duties to per-

The home of Mrs. Stevens, near Centreville, Virginia, was used as a hospital by Union forces during the First and Second Battles of Bull Run in 1861 and 1862.

Stretcher bearers practice loading patients onto a medical wagon. These early ambulances were used to cart the wounded to field hospitals set up some distance from the fighting.

form, and every officer has his place pointed out beforehand, and his duties defined, and held to a strict responsibility for their proper performance, the wounded must of course suffer.[26]

Letterman's understanding of the problem helped him devise a system to quickly remove wounded soldiers from battlefields. He also organized new types of medical facilities that allowed doctors to more efficiently treat soldiers. Under the Union army's Letterman Plan, each regiment trained soldiers as stretcher bearers to carry wounded from battle. Previously, sol-

diers had stopped fighting to take injured friends to safety, a practice that was haphazard and took many away from combat. The stretcher bearers' only job would be to help the wounded so that other soldiers could keep fighting. Letterman also assigned regiments horse-drawn ambulances to transport the wounded to hospitals.

Letterman's plan also ended confusion about where to treat soldiers by creating a hierarchy of medical facilities to care for them. Stretcher bearers carried the wounded first to nearby field stations, where doctors administered minimal emergency care. Ambulances then took seriously wounded soldiers to field hospitals, where surgeons performed amputations and other surgery. After being treated, wounded soldiers were finally transported by wagons, ships, or trains to general hospitals far from the fighting for long-term recuperation.

Letterman's system greatly improved medical care. It was in place for the Battle of Gettysburg in July 1863 when 14,193 Union soldiers were wounded over three days of fighting. Letterman's Gettysburg report included this comment from Surgeon John McNulty about how well his plan had worked: "It is with extreme satisfaction that I can assure you that it [the ambulance and hospital system] enabled me to remove the wounded from the field, shelter, feed them, and dress their wounds within six hours after the battle ended."[27]

The Confederates adopted similar measures to transport and treat soldiers.

EMERGENCY MEDICAL CARE

Under the Letterman Plan, the first stop for the wounded was so close to the fighting that they could still hear the roar of battle. Field stations were battlefield collection points that had to be located behind hills and rock formations or in deep gullies to shield them from errant rifle and cannon fire. Union surgeon John S. Billings once began treating soldiers in the shelter of a house only forty yards from a raging battle. To his chagrin, Billings discovered that the soldiers whom he was trying to help thought his field station was too near the fighting. Billings noted, "I soon found that the wounded who could walk would not stop where I was—it was entirely too close. [Even] the bearers of the badly wounded men would not stop, so I moved back about 200 yards and began to work there."[28]

Field stations had to be close to the battlefield so the wounded men could be treated as quickly as possible. Even though it was dangerous working so near the fighting, Confederate assistant surgeon William H. Taylor claimed doctors were willing to risk their lives to help soldiers:

It was on the battlefield that the assistant surgeon was in his own sphere, for it was the method of our service for him to be with the troops when they were in action, that he might render immediate aid to the wounded. Here he did his strenuous work. It was necessary for these stations to be near the engaged men [but] sometimes our only protection while ministering to a wounded man was by sitting, or even lying, with him on the ground.[29]

Field stations were manned by an assistant surgeon and a medical steward, an aide who carried medical supplies and helped treat the wounded. Doctors performed basic emergency care such as bandaging wounds, setting broken bones, and giving soldiers brandy, opium, or morphine to ease their pain. Doctors removed bullets only if they could easily extract them; more complex surgery was done in field hospitals.

The doctors' final task was to use triage—a method of evaluating wounds—to determine the order in which to send soldiers to field hospitals. Soldiers were grouped in three categories: those with minor injuries who could still walk; seriously injured soldiers who needed advanced care to survive; and soldiers with mortal wounds who were expected to die. Soldiers with serious wounds to the abdomen or chest were in the final category because doctors did not know how to treat such injuries. Union surgeon W.W. Keen said the only thing doctors could do for them was to ease their pain. "Opium was practically our only remedy," Keen remarked, "and death the usual result [of such wounds]."[30] The walking wounded and mortally wounded were sent to hospitals last so doctors could have a better chance of saving the others.

Surgeons affiliated with the U.S. Army Surgeon General's Office pose in front of their headquarters in Washington, D.C.

Sudley Church was used by Union doctors as a field hospital during the First Battle of Bull Run in July 1861. The interiors of such buildings were usually stripped to make room for surgeries.

The wounded made the journey to field hospitals in wagons. The trip was often painful as the ambulances bounced up and down on rough roads, but soldiers welcomed the harsh ride because they knew it could save their lives.

FIELD HOSPITALS

Field hospitals were located several miles from battle to ensure the safety of patients. Although doctors sometimes used large tents, they preferred to locate hospitals in homes, barns, and other permanent structures because they provided better shelter. Once a building had been chosen, doctors readied it for wounded soldiers who would soon be arriving. Union assistant surgeon D.S. Magruder explains how he converted an old stone church near Centreville, Virginia, into a hospital on July 21, 1861, after the First Battle of Bull Run: "I sent men to [remove] the seats . . . had the floor covered with what blankets could be found, buckets of water brought, instruments and dressings placed in convenient places for use, and operating tables improvised, and sent off men to the fields nearby to bring hay for bedding."[31]

As many more wounded arrived, Magruder had to use three other buildings as hospitals. Eventually they also became filled, and the remaining patients were sheltered outside under trees. This hospital overflow was common after big battles. In a letter, Confederate surgeon Spencer Glasgow Welch told his wife that near his field hospital, he once "saw large numbers of wounded lying on the ground as thick as a drove of hogs in a [farm] lot."[32]

Buildings and tents used for field hospitals provided little more than protection from the elements. There were no beds for patients, only hay or straw when it was available, and doctors had to improvise makeshift operating rooms to perform surgery. Doctors created operating tables by ripping doors off the hinges and propping them up with sawhorses or, if they were in a church, by laying wooden planks over the tops of pews. Because Confederate surgeon Archibald Atkinson Jr. was in the cavalry and always on the move, he carried his own operating table, a door that was specially equipped so it could be set up quickly. In his diary, Atkinson wrote, "[On it] 4 legs were

hinged [and] when a hospital was established [an aide] would bury the legs a foot in the ground [and] I had a good operating table."[33]

TYPES OF CARE

In field hospitals, doctors had more time and safer facilities in which to treat seriously wounded soldiers. Doctors removed bullets, bone fragments, and bits of metal from wounds, usually with their fingers but sometimes with long metal probes. After cleaning out debris and dirt, doctors sewed the wounds closed and applied bandages. The bandages were always wet because doctors believed the dampness promoted healing.

Tending to wounds sometimes involved delicate procedures that most doctors had never tried. For example, in May 1863 after the Battle of Chancellorsville, Union surgeon Billings operated on three soldiers, each of whom had been shot in the head. Doctors in this period rarely attempted such surgery because of their lack of knowledge of the brain, but Billings removed the bullets and saved the lives of the patients. Of the most difficult of the three operations, Billings wrote, "A ball had entered the cranium [and] penetrated the substance of the brain. I removed the ball, the fragments of bone and the letter of the man's cap, which had been forced into the interior [portion] of the brain [by the ball]."[34]

❧ WHERE TO PLACE A FIELD HOSPITAL ❧

When Dr. Richard Swanton Vickery completed his medical training in 1864 at the University of Michigan, he had already spent several years as a doctor with the Second Michigan Infantry. As a college thesis, Vickery wrote "On the Duties of the Surgeon in Action," which described how doctors tended soldiers wounded in battle. His thesis included how to choose a location for a field hospital. This excerpt from his thesis is from an article in the Civil War Times Illustrated.

It should be as secure as possible from shot and shell. In these days of rifled small arms and artillery, it cannot be out of range but by taking advantage of inequalities of the ground, getting behind some slight hill or knoll, comparative safety may be obtained and shelter from the heaviest fire: and there are few positions a Regiment can be in which a practiced eye will not discern some slight cover, close enough to be serviceable for that purpose. The advantages of this are that his [medical] attendants are cool and attentive to their duties, not watching the coming shot or shell with one eye and the patient with the other—that the wounded just in from the hot strife have a grateful feeling of safety, and are not agitated by seeing men fall around them—and last, not least, that the Surgeon himself, however brave, will be able to discharge his duty more clearly, steadily and quietly than if under direct fire.

Doctors did not treat many head wounds; about seven out of ten wounds they saw were to the arms and legs. This was because soldiers usually fought behind the shelter of trees or man-made fortifications and because soldiers with wounds in other parts of their bodies often died before reaching hospitals. Three-fourths of all wounds were caused by the soft-lead minié ball, which tore huge holes in the target's body and smashed apart bones and joints. Confederate surgeon Deering J. Roberts witnessed the terrible damage caused by minié balls.

In a book he wrote after the war with Union and Confederate doctors, Roberts explained,

These wounds differed in some important and very material characteristics from all gunshot wounds in preceding wars. The shattering, splintering, and splitting of a long bone by the impact of the minie were, in many instances, both remarkable and frightful, and early experience taught surgeons that amputation was the only means of saving life.[35]

The minié ball's destructive power was one of the main reasons that three out of every four surgeries in the war were amputations. Civil War doctors performed so many amputations that soldiers nicknamed them "sawbones" after the bone saws they used to sever damaged arms and legs.

AMPUTATIONS

Union medical records state that Northern surgeons performed 29,981 amputations, and it is estimated that Confederate doctors performed another 20,000. Doctors used saws resembling a modern-day hacksaw to sever everything from fingers to entire arms and legs. In a letter to his wife, Union surgeon Benjamin Woodward explained how busy he had been after one battle. Woodward wrote, "At the [field] hospital yesterday I helped amputate one foot and two legs and two arms and this afternoon I took off an arm above the elbow and one below. I have just taken off a middle finger at the last joint for Capt. Hubbard of this regiment."[36]

Everyone from privates to generals suffered amputations. Two high-ranking amputees were Confederate general John B. Hood, who survived removal of his right leg 4.5 inches from his hip, and Union major general Daniel E. Sickles, who lost his lower right leg. Sickles presented his severed leg bone to the Army Medical Museum in Washington, D.C., and for many years afterward he visited it on the anniversary of his amputation. It is still on display there today. Another noted amputee was Confederate Thomas "Stonewall" Jackson, who was accidentally shot three times by his own men on May 2, 1863, during the Battle of Chancellorsville. Jackson was taken to a field hospital in a tavern, where Surgeon Hunter McGuire cut off his left arm. Describing the operation, McGuire wrote:

> I told him that amputation would probably be required, and asked if it was found necessary whether it should be done at once. He replied promptly: "Yes, certainly. Dr. McGuire, do for me whatever you think best." The left arm was then amputated about two inches below the shoulder, very rapidly and with slight loss of blood.[37]

Jackson soon died because he had multiple injuries and became sick with pneumonia. Most patients lived, however, because an amputation was a quick, simple operation. Some surgeons could remove limbs in less than one minute. Amputations were also relatively painless because doctors almost always used ether or chloroform to put their patients to sleep.

In amputating a limb, doctors first applied a tourniquet on major arteries located above the amputation point to prevent blood loss. Using scalpels, doctors stripped away muscle and tissue to uncover the bone or joint and then cut through it with a saw. To prevent bleeding, doctors sewed shut large arteries that had been severed during the amputation. Finally, the doctors folded a flap of skin and muscle tissue over the amputation so that when it healed it would harden and create a stump, a thickened piece of skin and tissue that would become the end of the limb.

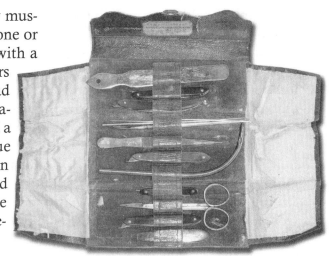

While most Union doctors carried a small surgical kit (above), commissioned Union surgeons possessed a larger carrying case (below) for their tools.

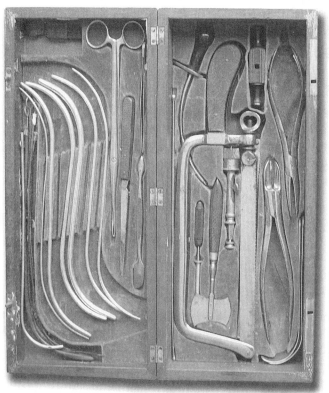

An alternative to amputation was resection. This was a more complicated operation in which doctors cut away part of the injured bone in an attempt to save the arm or leg. In a letter to his wife on June 13, 1863, during the siege of Vicksburg, Mississippi, Union surgeon John B. Rice boasted of his success in doing this kind of surgery on one of his patients. Rice asserted, "I resected the elbow in the case of J.L. Jackson [and] I have strong hopes of his entire recovery with a useful limb."[38]

Doctors generally chose amputation over resection. One reason was that removing part of the bone often left the limb useless because the leg or arm was not solid in its entire length. Amputations were also much simpler and quicker. This allowed doctors to treat more soldiers in a shorter time, which helped save more lives.

However, the soldiers who were losing arms or legs or feared losing a limb did not understand the medical reasons that led doctors to perform so many amputations. The result was that many soldiers criticized doctors for performing so many of them.

BUTCHERY OR GOOD MEDICINE?

One reason many soldiers feared amputations was that they often witnessed them up close. Because doctors often performed surgery outdoors or at the entrance of tents so they would have better lighting and fresh air, passing soldiers often saw the gory procedure. Private Wilbur Fisk of the Second Vermont Volunteers once saw an amputation. As Fisk recalled, "The surgeons, besmeared with blood, and hardened to their business, looked more like butchers cutting up beef than like professional men adopting the stern alternative of removing a limb to save the life of a fellow man."[39]

His vivid description shows why this type of surgery sickened soldiers. Union and Confederate soldiers also feared amputations because most jobs in this era required physical labor. A soldier who lost an arm or a leg would have trouble making a living after the war. Although doctors were aware that the future might be difficult for amputees, they performed thousands of amputations because they believed saving the soldier's life was their main concern. Amputation fit into their theory of conservative surgery, a term for operations done with the sole concern of keeping patients alive. Confederate surgeon Roberts explained this philosophy: "Conservative surgery was, I might say, almost, if not entirely, a universal principle with the Confederate surgeon; conservation, first, as to the life of the wounded soldier, secondly, as to his future comfort and usefulness."[40]

Doctors performed so many amputations because they knew that most

❧ A Mistake During Surgery ❧

W. W. Keen, one of the Union's finest surgeons, knew a lot more than many of the doctors whom he encountered in battlefield situations. In this excerpt from his memoirs, taken from the Web site of the Society of Civil War Surgeons, Keen explains how another doctor's lack of knowledge once threatened a patient's life:

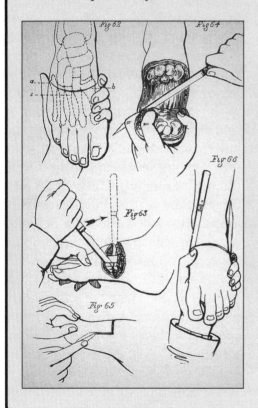

One of the wounded required an amputation at the shoulder-joint, and the operator [operating doctor] asked [another] surgeon to compress the subclavian artery. This he proceeded to do by vigorous pressure applied below the clavici [instead of above it]. With a good deal of hesitation I at last timidly suggested to him that possibly compression above the clavicle would be more efficacious, when, with withering scorn, he informed me that he was pressing in the right place, as was proved by the name of the artery, which was subclavian. I do not remember whether the operator took a hand in this little linguistic discussion or even overheard it. I had my rather grim revenge, happily, not to the serious disadvantage of the patient. When the operator made the internal flap [for a stump] the artery gave one enormous jet of blood, for the subclavian persisted in running where it could be compressed above the clavicle in spite of its name. I caught the artery in the flap, as I had been taught to do, and instantly controlled the hemorrhage.

A plate from Moore's Manual, a Confederate surgeon's guide, shows the proper method of foot amputation.

soldiers would die if they did not have surgery, either from the injury itself or from infections that almost always began in shattered limbs that were not severed. The failure of soldiers and the public to understand this led many to criticize doctors. After the Battle of Antietam in September 1862, Union surgeon Letterman jumped to the defense of his doctors after hearing and reading negative comments about the high number of amputations:

> The surgery of these battle-fields has been pronounced butchery. Gross misrepresentations of the conduct of medical officers have been made. It is not to be supposed that there were no incompetent surgeons in the army. It is certainly true that there were [but] if any objection could be urged against the surgery of those fields, it would be the efforts on the part of surgeons to practice "conservative surgery" to too great an extent. I am convinced that if any fault was committed it was that the knife was not used enough.[41]

The doctors who made the difficult decision to amputate were the best physicians either side had. Union surgeon George T. Stevens explained after the war that only the most qualified doctors—they were called

A Union surgeon holds a knife in preparation for surgery at a field hospital. Not every military doctor was entrusted with the task of performing major operations.

♪ A COMPASSIONATE CONFEDERATE DOCTOR ♭

Confederate surgeon Archibald Atkinson Jr. was one of many Civil War surgeons who tried to avoid performing amputations whenever possible. In a Civil War memoir he wrote, which is now posted on the Web site of the Virginia Tech University Libraries, Atkinson describes how he saved two men from losing limbs:

Joe [Webb] begged me not to let his leg be cut off. I told him I would do my best [and] asked him if it would save his life would he be willing to lose leg—he said "no." I found his knee was pierced by a minnie ball but that the chances were as good to get well with a stiff joint as that he should die. So I won the day [and] saved Joe's leg.

. . . [Major Johnathan] W. Daniel of Lynchburg was brought with his right thigh bone fractured. We examined him [and] the consensus of opinion was that to save his life he should lose his thigh high up. Dr. Grimes [and] I fought against it contending that for a man to lose his thigh at that point even if he recovered his life would be a burden. We gained our point [and] finding the bone very much shattered we enlarged the bullet wound sufficiently to pick out all loose bits of crushed bones [and] rounded up the pointed ends of the fractured parts, [and] he recovered finally the use of his leg. I saved a good many limbs [and] all did well as far as I know.

"operating surgeons" or "operators"—were allowed to perform major surgery. "It was a mistaken impression among those at home," Stevens said, "that each [unit's doctor] was the operating surgeon for his own men. Only about one in fifteen of the [army's doctors present at a battle] was entrusted with operations."[42]

DOING SURGERY AFFECTED DOCTORS

Even though doctors knew amputations saved lives, doing so many operations was hard on them. After the Battle of Perryville in Kentucky on October 8, 1862, Confederate surgeon Charles Quintard explained in a letter to his wife how drained he was mentally and physically after long hours of amputating limbs and performing surgery. Quintard wrote, "About half past five in the morning of the 9th, I dropped—I could do no more. I went out by myself and leaning against a fence, I wept like a child. And all that day I was so unnerved that if anyone asked me about the regiment, I could make no reply without tears."[43]

CHAPTER 3

DOCTORS ON THE BATTLEFIELD

Union and Confederate doctors in field stations were often in danger because they worked so near the fighting. While stationed on a Virginia battlefield, Confederate assistant surgeon Isaac White explained in a letter to his wife, Jinnie, that it was frightening to be so close to combat. "It is terrible to hear the constant roar of cannon [and] musketry [and] to know that we are in so much danger,"[44] White admitted. The danger White wrote about was a constant threat to battlefield surgeons. In his official report after the Battle of Gettysburg, Union surgeon Jonathan Letterman noted that thirteen doctors had been wounded and one killed. Letterman commented dryly that "the idea, very prevalent [among soldiers and civilians], that medical officers are not exposed to fire, is thus shown to be wholly erroneous."[45]

Union records indicate that at least fifty doctors were killed during battles or were wounded and died afterward. At least another three hundred died from other causes, mainly diseases such as typhoid fever and malaria. Because Confederate records are incomplete, it is not known how many Southern doctors lost their lives. Confederate surgeon Hunter Holmes McGuire, however, claims many doctors died bravely in battle:

One, I saw fall at Strasburg, amid the cheers of soldiers at the evidence he gave of devotion to duty. Another, at Sharpsburg, facing an assault before which even veterans quailed and fled, and a third I found upon the bloody field of Cold Harbor dying with a shell-wound through his side. As I knelt down beside him and told him his wound was mortal, he answered, "I am no more afraid to die than I was afraid to do my duty."[46]

It was not always wounds that imperiled the lives of doctors, who were susceptible to the same physical ailments as other soldiers. For example, while retreating from a battle in May 1864, Union doctor John G. Perry suffered heatstroke and almost died before an aide helped him. In describing the incident to his wife, Perry wrote, "My steward says that while on the retreat I talked incoherently, then ran and shouted until he guided me to the Hospital where I fell unconscious."[47]

TENDING WOUNDS IN BATTLE

Although combat doctors usually treated injured soldiers in field stations located in protected spots, they sometimes ventured onto battlefields to tend the wounded. Doctors did this

This painting of the Battle of Fredericksburg, Virginia, in December 1862 shows Union surgeons performing amputations in front of nervous troops that have yet to march into battle.

even though they knew it meant they would be in as much danger from musket and cannon fire as the soldiers they treated. Union surgeon Alfred Lewis Castleman said it did not take him long to realize the danger when he ventured into battle in September 1862 to tend the wounded. "Whilst I administered to their wants," Castleman wrote, "the bullets of the enemy's passing in unpleasant proximity admonished me that I was [in danger]."[48]

Doctors braved battlefields to help soldiers by stopping their wounds from bleeding, easing their pain, and helping them to safety. Sometimes, however, they came too late to help a wounded soldier. This happened to Union surgeon Benjamin Woodward, who ventured into the middle of the fighting to answer the painful pleas of a mortally wounded comrade. Woodward recalled:

> One poor fellow called to me (he was of our regiment and knew me well) "Doctor help me!" . . . I ran to him, a cannon ball had torn his bowels all open and his intestines were hanging in shreds. [Realizing the man would shortly die] I just poured a mouthful of brandy in his mouth from my canteen and left him. A few minutes after, I saw him dead.[49]

Many doctors showed extreme bravery while tending the wounded in such

situations. After one battle in 1862, artillery officer James Thompson praised Medical Cadet Frank Le Moyne for risking his life to care for wounded men while fighting raged about him. As Thompson wrote, "[Le Moyne] was on the field of battle or near [our position] during the entire day, and worked until late at night dressing [bandaging and cleaning wounds] wounded until all were attended to. His conduct deserves great commendation."[50]

Some doctors, however, fled in panic when bullets began whizzing around them. In a letter to his wife dated October 24, 1863, Surgeon White complained of how some colleagues acted during a battle near Charleston, Virginia. As White wrote, "I can say truthfully that the surgeons of this command are the grandest cowards I ever saw. Not one remained with me on the field [to help the wounded]. I don't believe they stopped running under 12 miles."[51]

Most doctors, however, learned to handle fear even though many of them were not exposed to danger regularly. In September 1861, Castleman was left alone near a battlefield in Virginia with wounded soldiers while another doctor went for help to move them. Castleman remembered how he dealt with his fear:

> I confess that as I caught the last glimpse of the [doctor's] fine black horse dashing over the hill, there

was at the ends of my fingers and toes a sensation very much akin to the "oozing out of courage." I was alone in the enemy's country. But there was no other way now, so I dressed the wounds, and waited his return, with what patience I could.[52]

Even when doctors found themselves in the middle of a battle, they generally did not take part in the fighting because they were too busy trying to save lives. At times, however, some doctors became caught up in the emotions of combat. This happened to Confederate surgeon Simon Baruch, who was dismayed when he saw soldiers fleeing from a Union attack during a large battle. Baruch explains how he unsuccessfully tried to convince his fellow soldiers to quit running and start fighting again:

> At the close of the Battle of Cedar Run I foolishly undertook with a colleague to check the flight of a group of soldiers when I saw General [Jubal] Early with waving flag imploring the men to stop the rout. Galloping towards the front I yelled, "Rally, men, for God's sake, rally." A shell exploded over my head, and my horse took the bit and ran away. The men [surprised he was heading the wrong way] yelled after me, "Why in hell don't you rally?"[53]

LONG-RANGE DANGER

The battlefield, however, was not the only place doctors were in danger. Artillery guns could fire shells for several miles, which meant surgeons in field hospitals far from battle could be killed or wounded. At the Battle of Gettysburg, Confederate assistant surgeon William H. Taylor suffered a deep gash several inches long in one leg when artillery shells struck his hospital. Taylor described the scene when the shells landed: "In a moment the air was filled with limbs of trees, scraps of [metal food pots] and yells of fleeing medical men and knapsack-toters [soldiers]."[54] Such artillery attacks were so common that some doctors became used to them. Confederate surgeon Spencer Glasgow Welch wrote in his diary June 16, 1862, that "the enemy threw shells all about our camp yesterday and killed two horses, but only one man."[55]

Confederate surgeon Herbert M. Nash also experienced many extended artillery duels across Virginia's Rappahannock River, which physically separated the Union and Confederate forces but posed no barrier to cannon fire. During one bombardment, Nash and a young soldier assigned to help him tend some wounded soldiers had to dash across a road to safety. The two tried to time their runs to avoid the incoming shells, but one missile struck his assistant. Nash explains the sad outcome:

❧ A DOCTOR BECOMES A SOLDIER ❧

Although doctors were generally not expected to do anything but care for sick and wounded soldiers, they sometimes had to perform military tasks. This happened once to Confederate surgeon Herbert M. Nash, who was ordered to stop soldiers from leaving the battle line after a fierce Union attack. Nash's description of the incident is taken from the Web site of the Society of Civil War Surgeons:

On another occasion a severe fusillade [exchange of shots] broke out on the picket lines [the edge of the battle] and demoralized men came in reporting our lines broken [the enemy had run through them]. The General's aides had been sent off on other duty, and being near him, he ordered me to go to the front, ascertain the real condition, and report to him. I merely remarked as I went that this was novel duty for a surgeon, trudged through the mud in the darkness, and expecting to be shot every minute by the excited men for a Yankee [Union soldier], soon found both ends of the broken lines, urged the officers to close them up, and returned to report, and received an apology from the General for having sent me on such a unpleasant duty. In all subsequent engagements he cared for my personal safety by directing me to a sheltered position when the firing became hot, that I might perform my duties with more serenity of mind.

Watching the flash of the [Union] guns, I ran across safely, but my poor drummer boy followed me too closely, was struck by a shell, tearing and lacerating his left thigh, causing him to sink rapidly into shock and death, giving me great distress as I watched the ebbing away of his brave little life.[56]

Doctors could also be endangered by enemy snipers, sharpshooters who could accurately hit individuals several hundred yards away. Snipers usually aimed at officers, including doctors, because their loss would be felt more deeply than the death of common soldiers. David Warman, a Union contract surgeon who normally worked at a large hospital far from combat, once visited the front so he could view the fighting. His curiosity about war, however, almost cost him his life. In his diary for August 1864, Warman explained how he was nearly shot while standing next to a group of officers overlooking a battlefield:

The firing and skirmishing was incessant. In my curiosity to look at Rebels and sharpshooters, I mounted the outer earth works [barricade] and pulled out my field glass to have a good look at them when a mini ball was fired at me and struck in the earth at my feet. A little higher and it would have gone through my body. . . . We found the vicinity rather hot and uncomfortable and concluded to vacate.[57]

Warman was nearly shot because he got too close to the site of an ongoing battle. Many doctors, however, found that danger came to them courtesy of the constant ebb and flow of combat between two armies.

SHIFTING BATTLE LINES

Soldiers for both armies ranged far and wide around the sites of major battles. Depending on which side was winning, large numbers of soldiers would advance forward or retreat backward hundreds of yards or even several miles. In addition, bands of

A medical team treats a soldier for a leg injury in a field hospital. The assistant behind the table holds cotton soaked with chloroform or another anesthetic.

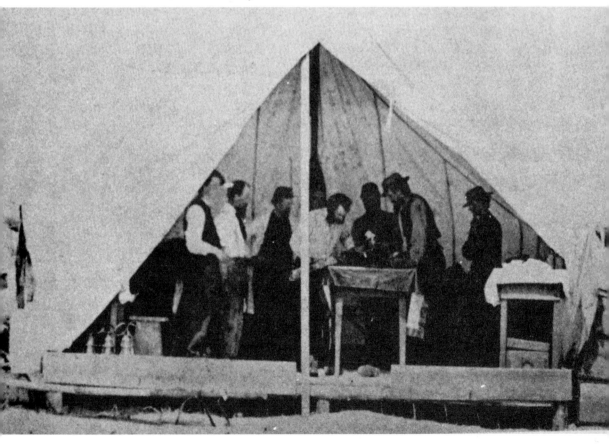

cavalry and other military units usually operated around the periphery of the main battlefield to strike at an enemy's flank or rear. In this larger zone of warfare, no one was ever entirely secure because enemy soldiers could appear at any minute and attack them. This included doctors working in hospitals.

In July 1864, during several days of combat for possession of Kennesaw Mountain near Atlanta, Georgia, battle lines changed constantly. Because of this, doctors had to keep moving to avoid the enemy. In his diary for July 1, Union surgeon John W. Foye commented, "The field hospital was moved seven times to accommodate itself to the ranging [shifting] positions of the command."[58] Confederate surgeon Taylor experienced the same disruption in performing his duties in another battle, noting, "We shifted our [medical] stations, when it became necessary, to conform to the movements of the fighting line."[59]

Doctors on both sides moved hospitals to ensure the safety of wounded soldiers and to prevent the enemy from stealing their medical supplies, a common occurrence because both sides often ran short of such items. Sometimes, however, doctors could not move fast enough to avoid enemy advances. This happened to Union surgeon W.W. Keen in August 1862 during the Second Battle of Bull Run, when a Confederate cavalry unit over-

ran his hospital. Keen said the Confederates, who were often short of medical supplies, were amazed at the treasure trove of medicines, bandages, and other things they found, including alcohol, which was used to ease the pain of wounded soldiers. In a speech decades later Keen said, "I have a very vivid recollection how their eyes widened and their faces were wreathed in smiles as the doctor, after a rapid survey of the boxes on the walls, turned to the colonel and said, with an expletive: 'There is more good whiskey in this little smoke-house than there is in the whole city of Richmond.'"[60] Although the Confederates took most of the supplies, they left enough for Keen to treat wounded soldiers. The reason for this was that doctors on both sides were willing to care for enemy soldiers, and the Confederates wanted to make sure that the Union doctors had proper supplies to treat injured Southerners.

HELPING THE ENEMY
For Union and Confederate doctors, there were no enemies. Doctors from both sides gave the same treatment to wounded enemy soldiers as they did their own. In a college thesis he wrote about the duties of a military doctor, Union surgeon Richard Swanton Vickery eloquently explained the philosophy underlying this humane war practice: "If any wounded of the enemy are brought

in, they should receive all the care and attention the Surgeon can possibly pay them consistent with his duty to his own men, who have the first claim upon his time. When a man is struck down he ceases to be an enemy and becomes a patient."[61]

When the fighting ended, doctors from both armies fanned out over the still smoke-covered battlefields to help all soldiers regardless of the uniform they wore. Wounded soldiers taken prisoner were also treated in field hospitals. After the Confederate victory at the Second Battle of Bull Run in August 1862, for example, doctors from both sides helped treat a large number of wounded Union soldiers. In his official report Surgeon Thomas McPharlin, medical director of the Army of the Potomac in 1864, wrote, "Surgeons were left in parties to care for wounded with what supplies they had, working with Confederate medical officers and assistants. I am happy to say that the Confederate soldiers shared with our wounded their scanty store [of medical supplies]."[62]

Union doctors showed the same kindness toward Confederate wounded. After a battle in Virginia in May 1862, Union assistant surgeon Alexander Ingram explained how Union doctors worked with Confederate doctors to treat hundreds of Southerners: "A number of amputations and a few extractions of balls were performed, the Union and Confederate surgeons working very amicably together."[63] The Confederate doctors Ingram mentioned had been taken prisoner. But when the soldiers had all been treated, they were set free.

DOCTORS AS PRISONERS OF WAR

The practice of treating doctors as noncombatants who should not be held as prisoners of war began after the Battle of Winchester on May 31, 1862. After the fight, Confederate surgeon Hunter Holmes McGuire convinced his superiors to release seven Union doctors by arguing that they would pose no harm to Confederates if they were freed. His argument so impressed Union army general George McClellan that he decided to follow McGuire's lead. On June 6 McClellan issued his own order declaring doctors should not be held prisoner. The order was in effect for the rest of the war.

At times, however, doctors did suffer at least minor abuse when they were captured. In May 1864 Union surgeon John G. Perry was held briefly as a prisoner. After being freed, Perry wrote to his wife about his experience: "Surgeons captured by the enemy are well treated and immediately [released]. But if one happens to have on a good pair of boots, he is generally relieved of them, which, under the circumstances, seems quite fair and proper."[64]

▪ A CAPTURED DOCTOR IS RESCUED ▪

Union surgeon Napoleon B. Brisbine was held as a prisoner for five weeks after being captured in August 1864 in Winchester, Virginia. In this letter reprinted on the Web site of the Virginia Military Institute, Brisbine explains the joy he felt when his Union soldiers freed him:

I was a prisoner five weeks to the day our troops recaptured me at this place. . . . All day the cannon bellowed and once in a while a breeze would bring the faint report of firearms, rifles, muskets, and carbines. But along in the afternoon, the small arms became quite plain and at length cheers could be heard, and a shell would come over me from the Yankee [side]. Then com-menced one of the greatest panic retreats I ever saw without any exception, and the [Confederate] horses, mules & men all went along with their tails up (excuse the last remark, the latter's tails were down). The old 8th Corps done wonders in that day and redeemed itself from all other stains. While the rebels were retreating through town a shell from one of our [cannons] came through our Hospital, going over two beds and striking the third one smashing it to splinters, tearing the straw out of the mattress and disappeared through the other side of the house, not hurting a man. The bed was occupied by a man with a fractured thigh but was not hurt.

Although they were not considered prisoners of war, doctors were sometimes held for a short time until an exchange of prisoners could be made. When Union surgeon Napoleon B. Brisbine was captured in 1864, he was held captive long enough to write a letter to his family. He explained to them that he had fallen into the hands of the Confederates during a battle in Winchester, Virginia, because he was doing his duty to care for the wounded:

On our retreat down the valley it fell to the lot of someone to stay with our wounded and that unfortunate one was your humble servant N.B.B. I had gone on through the place some eight miles [but then] received orders to go back immediately. I had just time to get here when the rebels came in and I was a prisoner.[65]

Brisbine was freed five weeks later, when Union troops recaptured Winchester. Another Union doctor was not so lucky and had to spend four months in a Southern prison. The doctor was Mary Edwards Walker, one of only two female doctors in the

Civil War and the first woman to earn the Medal of Honor, the nation's highest military award.

WALKER'S SECRET MISSION

When the war began, Walker, one of only a handful of female doctors in the nation, was turned down when she volunteered to be a Union surgeon. But the pressing need for more physicians helped her win a position in

A woman who often dressed in men's clothing, Mary Edwards Walker poses with the Medal of Honor pinned to her lapel in this 1865 photograph.

February 1862 as a contract surgeon for the Fifty-second Ohio Volunteers. The job Walker worked so hard to get became dangerous when her superiors decided to use her as a spy. Doctors during the war were allowed to pass through enemy lines to care for wounded prisoners and ill civilians. On such trips, doctors sometimes learned things that would help their side, such as enemy troop strengths. This informal spying was generally overlooked.

But after Walker made repeated journeys into Confederate areas beginning in late 1863, Confederates began to suspect what she was doing and arrested her on April 10, 1864, near Chattanooga, Tennessee.

Walker spent four months in a filthy, rat-infested prison before being released. By that time, malnutrition from poor food had weakened her eyes so much that they troubled her the rest of her life. After the war, President Andrew Johnson awarded Walker the Medal of Honor. The official recommendation for the medal stated, "[Walker] frequently passed beyond our lines far within those of the enemy, and at one time gained information that led General [William] Sherman to so modify his strategic operations as to save himself

✑ HIDING FROM THE ENEMY ✑

Doctors often had to hide from advancing enemy soldiers. In a memoir of his war years, now posted on the Virginia Tech University Libraries Internet site, Confederate surgeon Archibald Atkinson Jr. explains the difficult conditions he once had to endure to evade Union forces:

We knew the enemy were making for some new point, maybe only seeking for an open field or less dense wilderness or trying to hide their maneuvers. [To hide] we had to attend to our wounded in the midst of undergrowth so thick that we could scarcely move around, [and] no water to be had for washing off the wounded. There was a dearth of every thing except bullets, smoke [and] suffering. There was a sort of improvised bush hospital gotten up by Dr. Grimes [and] myself, but we could not even get our ambulance wagons to bring us supplies for operating [and] dressing wounds. . . . It was very hot weather [and] the close brush of woods composed of small [trees] 12 to 20 ft. high [and] rather larger than a man's arm made the heat almost suffocating. Added to this the smoke from burning powder [and] leaves made every breath an effort. It was almost impossible to distinguish friend from foe. The firing was terrific [and] the carnage awful. The thirst was almost unbearable [and] the whole surface of the earth afire with burning leaves.

from serious reverse and obtain success where defeat seemed to be inevitable."[66]

It took courage for Walker to spy for her country, and she had more than many male Civil War soldiers.

FEAR OR ILLNESS?

On September 14, 1862, during the Battle of South Mountain in Maryland, Confederate surgeon Simon Baruch was assigned to the rear guard, soldiers who were held back from initial fighting so they could be sent into combat when needed. During sick call, Baruch noticed a new illness among some soldiers. Baruch later commented, "When the booming of cannon became distinct, the number of sick soldiers increased, and when the rattling of musketry was heard they became unmanageable. Here I was confronted with a new disease. I would call it 'battlesickness.'"[67]

Baruch was only joking about having discovered a new illness. He realized that fear of combat led some soldiers to pretend they were sick so they could avoid fighting. That was just one of many things doctors learned by working so close to the fighting that they were often in danger themselves.

CHAPTER 4

STAFFING CIVIL WAR HOSPITALS

The first great battle of the Civil War was the First Battle of Bull Run, which was fought on July 21, 1861, near a railway junction in Manassas, Virginia. The Union suffered about three thousand casualties in the heavy fighting, and the Confederates incurred nearly two thousand casualties. The Confederates were victorious, sending Union soldiers fleeing north to nearby Washington, D.C. The aftermath of the battle was grim, however, because the Confederates had no hospitals in which to treat wounded soldiers. Confederate surgeon Edward Warren later described the haphazard way in which the injured were housed in any space available for miles around the scene of battle:

[They were] scattered through hotels, private houses, public halls and wherever it was possible to spread a blanket. In fact, from

what I could gather, the whole country, from Manassas Junction to Richmond in one direction, and to Lynchburg in another, was one vast hospital, filled to repletion with the sick and wounded of [the] victorious army.[68]

The Union faced the same problem. In one of the war's most disorganized retreats, thousands of wounded soldiers were carried by comrades or stumbled on their own power back to Washington, D.C., which was only thirty miles away. When the injured soldiers arrived, they discovered to their dismay that the city's two military hospitals could house only a few hundred wounded. Beleaguered medical officers sheltered soldiers in warehouses, private homes, and government buildings, including the partially completed Capitol, which today houses Congress. Wealthier soldiers with

❧ A Confederate Battle Hospital ❧

Transforming public buildings into hospitals after large battles was a difficult task for Civil War doctors. In March 1865 Confederate surgeon Simon Baruch was ordered to create a brigade hospital in Thomasville, North Carolina, to care for soldiers wounded in the Battle of Averysboro. In a letter reprinted in an article in Civil War Times Illustrated *magazine, Baruch explains how he had to rush to get the facility ready:*

I had built a bake oven and cleaned out some factories and a hotel, when I received a telegram announcing that 280 wounded were on their way to Thomasville. I immediately sent out an armed guard to bring all the men and large boys [from the city] to headquarters and impress them with the fact that they must assist me in my necessarily hasty preparations. I commandeered two wagons, put two men on each, and sent one to gather pine straw, the other to gather pine knots. I commandeered a large number of girls from a female college to fill all the straw sacks I had with pine straw [as mattresses] and lay them neatly on the floor of the building I had prepared. I went personally from house to house and obtained assistance from the women in baking bread and preparing coffee and bacon for the expected wounded. Next I had piles of pine knots placed in front of the building, which, when lighted, illuminated the town so that when the train arrived the wounded could be comfortably unloaded into the factories and two churches which I had emptied of pews, etc.

Confederates use fence rails and tent canvas to erect a makeshift field hospital at Antietam, Maryland, in September 1862.

minor injuries checked into hotels and hired civilian doctors to tend their wounds.

Bull Run was significant in the Civil War's medical history because it showed both sides that they needed large hospitals to care for the huge numbers of wounded soldiers the conflict would produce. North and South soon began building facilities in which doctors would save the lives of thousands of soldiers over the next four years.

A NEW CONCEPT

It is not surprising that the combatants failed to realize they would need large hospitals. Prior to the war, the U.S. Army had never needed such facilities because it rarely stationed many soldiers in any one place. Military outposts functioned with small infirmaries in which doctors could care for a few sick or wounded soldiers. In addition, there were few hospitals anywhere in America be-

cause most sick people were treated in a doctor's office or at home, often by a family member or a friend who had some skill in caring for sick people. Thus, a hospital that housed hundreds and even thousands of patients was a novel idea to Confederate and Union doctors.

The Civil War, however, quickly forced both sides to create large hospitals to provide long-term health care for sick and wounded soldiers. There were two types of such medical centers—brigade hospitals, temporary facilities located near major battles, and general hospitals, permanent structures

During the Battle of Cedar Mountain in August 1862, this farmhouse was converted into a Confederate brigade hospital. The loitering soldiers indicate that the hospital is situated a safe distance from the fighting.

placed in cities far from the fighting in which soldiers could spend weeks and even months recuperating from illness or wounds.

Such hospitals were new in civilian as well as military medical care, and they served as models for postwar facilities throughout the world. As Union surgeon John S. Billings once boasted, "We taught Europe how to build, organize, and manage hospitals."[69]

BRIGADE HOSPITALS

After being treated at field hospitals, soldiers were taken to larger, better-staffed facilities farther from the scene of battle. These medical centers were called brigade hospitals because they served an entire brigade, a military unit that encompassed several regiments. Brigade hospitals were usually located in warehouses, hotels, and other large buildings that army officials commandeered. When no permanent structures were available, brigade hospitals were created by erecting row after row of tents to house patients and medical facilities. Union surgeon Alfred Lewis Castleman described the hospital tents he was responsible for in Virginia: "My hospital at present consists of five large tents, fourteen feet long by fifteen feet wide. They open into each other at the ends, so as to make of the whole one long continuous tent, seventy feet long. This will accommodate forty patients comfortably. In an emergency I can crowd in fifty-five."[70]

Brigade hospitals were needed after large battles. Doctors there performed additional surgery on severely injured soldiers and checked to make sure their wounds were healing properly. In addition, when large numbers of soldiers became ill with diseases such as typhoid fever and malaria, they were sent to brigade hospitals because they had more doctors, stewards, and nurses to care for them. Soldiers who recovered were sent back to their units. Patients whose wounds would take longer to heal or were seriously ill were transported to general hospitals for long-term medical care.

Doctors in charge of brigade hospitals were responsible for other tasks besides just caring for sick and wounded soldiers. For example, they needed to feed their patients nourishing food so they would get well. Because it was often difficult in a war zone to get enough food, doctors often had to use their ingenuity to feed their patients. In a diary entry, Confederate surgeon Archibald Atkinson Jr. explained his solution for providing meals for almost five hundred sick and convalescent soldiers in the hospital he had set up in a large hotel: "We had the poorest commissary [food supply] arrangements, [and] all I could get for my men was salt [and] hard crackers. I made the convalescents [recovering patients] shoot squirrels, ground hogs, pheasants, [and] turkeys [and] I made all sorts of soups [and] stews for the men."[71]

Patients in brigade hospitals usually enjoyed other amenities, such as beds and bathing facilities. However, the general hospitals both sides built for long-term patient care had much more to offer patients in terms of comfort and medical care.

GENERAL HOSPITALS

During the Civil War, the Union and Confederate armies engaged in the greatest hospital construction boom the nation had ever seen. The Union built 192 general hospitals, and the Confederacy erected at least 154. They were called general hospitals because they received patients from any regiment or brigade. The Washington, D.C., area was home to about 85 hospitals. Although the nation's capital had a population of only seventy-five thousand, area military hospitals could house fifty thousand patients.

Washington became a medical center because so many of the war's major battles occurred in nearby Virginia. Its proximity to the same conflicts also turned Richmond, Virginia, the Confederacy's capital, into the South's chief medical center. By early 1864 Richmond had twenty hospitals, including Chimborazo, whose capacity of more than eight thousand patients when it opened on October 11, 1862, made it the largest military medical facility that had ever been built. The Union also constructed several huge medical centers including hospitals in New York and Philadelphia that each held more than five thousand patients.

At the start of the war, general hospitals were often housed in existing buildings. However, converting warehouses, hotels, college dormitories, and even churches to medical use was a difficult task. Union surgeon W.W. Keen discovered this in May 1862 when he was ordered to transform Ascension Episcopal Church and Eighth Street Methodist Church in Washington, D.C., into medical facilities. Keen recalled:

> To get those two churches ready as hospitals I had to have beds, mattresses, sheets, pillow-cases, chairs, tables, kitchen utensils, knives, forks, spoons, peppers and salts, all sorts of crockery, and the other necessities for a dining-room; all the drugs, appliances, and [medical] instruments needed for a drug-store for two hundred sick and wounded men. I did not know how to get a single one of these requisites.[72]

The task facing Keen was even more difficult because he was ordered to transform the churches into hospitals in just five days. Working nearly around the clock while sleeping only a few hours each night, the young

The sprawling complex of buildings comprising Chimborazo Hospital in Richmond, Virginia, shows why Chimborazo was the largest medical facility of its time.

doctor somehow managed to finish his hurried preparations in only three days. "On the fourth day," Keen proudly noted, "I had one hundred wounded men in each hospital."[73]

As the war progressed, both sides built scores of general hospitals. Specifically designed as medical centers, they had many features that would help patients recover.

PAVILION HOSPITALS

Most Civil War general hospitals were patterned after the pavilion style, an architectural layout that separated patients into wards. This was done by constructing wings, called pavilions,

which branched off from the central part of the hospital. The wings, which in Union hospitals could extend up to 120 feet, contained individual wards to house patients. In a book he wrote after the war, Union surgeon Edward L. Munson described this style of construction: "The wards radiate like the spokes of a wheel from a covered passageway which extends completely around the [central hub of the] hospital. Inside this circle was a bakery, laundry, offices, and rooms for the surgeons [to work]."[74]

Most Confederate hospitals followed this pavilion pattern, although their wings were usually a little shorter. The wings in both Confederate and Union hospitals were about fifteen feet wide; beds faced inward from each wall, leaving a corridor between them. Toilets and bathing facilities were located at the end of each wing. Some hospitals even had modern toilets that used water to flush waste away instead of collecting it in a latrine-style container.

The wings were designed with large windows and openings in the ceilings and floors so fresh air could flow freely through them. This is how Confederate surgeon Samuel H. Stout, who was in charge of hospitals in Georgia, described this ventilation system: "Near the floor, and just under the ceiling overhead, were openings with sliding shutters one foot in width that could be closed or opened at the will of the surgeon in charge. Overhead, in the ceiling, were also openings with sliding shutters [that] were opened or closed as occasion required."[75]

The most elaborate Civil War hospital was Chimborazo, which had 150 separate wings and outbuildings. During the war, this enormous facility treated more than seventy-six thousand soldiers. The Chimborazo complex in-

The tidied ward of a Union hospital in Washington, D.C., reveals the typical length of a wing in Union pavilion-style general hospitals.

cluded five soup houses, five icehouses, a bakery that produced ten thousand loaves of bread each day, and an adjacent farm to provide food and milk. Feeding soldiers well was one of the top priorities of big hospitals. Confederate surgeon W.G. Stevenson once boasted that at his hospital in Selma, Alabama, "Wines, jellies, strawberries [and] cakes were always abundant."[76]

Even without such delicacies, food and hospital life in general were so good compared to being in the field that many injured or sick soldiers tried to stay in them after they had recovered. In a letter to his family, Union surgeon John Alexander Ritter complained about how hard it was to get some soldiers to return to their units: "They play old soldier from the start. They get in to a hospital and they stay their [sic] always. . . . [They] are a great drawback to the service and there are many more of them than one would suppose."[77]

Doctors lucky enough to be assigned to hospitals also enjoyed more comforts than physicians in camps, on the march, or in battle. David Warman was a Union contract surgeon at Chesapeake Hospital in Virginia. Although Warman complained in his diary that he had to pay for his own meals, he was delighted with the room he had near the hospital. Said Warman, "We had all the comforts of city life in the Brown Cottage, as it was called, such as bath tub and shower bath. We had a large room and a good spring bed. I began to feel almost at home."[78]

Hospital Work

Doctors assigned to hospitals had a wide range of duties. They visited patients daily to check on their progress, prescribed medicine, and performed surgery. For the most part, doctors easily handled this routine work. On November 13, 1863, Union surgeon Washington Nugent wrote to his wife that he was becoming comfortable in his new position at Fort Delaware Hospital, one of many facilities in Northern states like Delaware. "The duties in general," Nugent wrote, "are not arduous, I visit my ward of fifty patients at [8:30] in the mornings, at 4 in the afternoon and as often between times as I feel disposed. I prescribe [medicine] for them, fix the diet table and order whatever I please in regard to arrangement of my patients."[79]

However, the duties of hospital doctors were often much more demanding. When new patients arrived, physicians had to examine each wounded or ill soldier and determine a course of treatment. In addition, hospitals close to battle sites sometimes received wounded soldiers direct from combat and therefore had to contend quickly with a flood of injured men. Esther Hill Hawks was a

❧ A FEMALE DOCTOR ❧

Esther Hill Hawks was a Union contract surgeon. She and her husband, Milton Hawks, who was also a doctor, cared for African American soldiers and civilians in Hilton Head, South Carolina. In addition to working in General Hospital Number 10, Hawks briefly served as the doctor for a black infantry unit. In A Woman Doctor's Civil War: Esther Hill Hawks' Diary, *edited by Gerald Schwartz, Hill explains the resistance she met from some soldiers at having a female doctor examine them:*

Meanwhile no surgeon being sent to take charge of the hospital, I am left manager of not only the affairs of the hospital, but have to attend Surgeons' [sick] call for the 2nd Regiment [of South Carolina Volunteers]—so every morning at 9 o'clock the disabled are marched down to the hospital in charge of a Sergeant and I hold Surgeon's call [and] with great success. An occasional chronic "shirk" [a soldier pretending to be sick] will complain to the Colonel [Robert Shaw] that, "Dat woman ca'nt do me no gud, she ca'nt see my pain" but he gets no sympathy from the Colonel and is obliged to go on duty if I so mark him. So for three weeks I performed the duties of hospital and Regimental Surgeon doing the work so well that the neglect to supply a regular officer was not discovered at [headquarters].

Union contract surgeon in General Hospital Number 10 in Beaufort, South Carolina. She is one of only two women known to have worked as a Civil War doctor. Hawks worked feverishly for hours to treat members of the Fifty-fourth Massachusetts Colored Infantry after their most famous battle, a valiant but failed attempt to capture Morris Island. In her diary, Hawks wrote about the nonstop surgery she performed:

It was a busy time, and the amount of work done in that 24 hours by the two [male] surgeons, and one woman is tiresome to remember! The only thing that sustained us was the patient endurance of those stricken heroes lying before us, with their ghastly wounds cheerful & courageous, many a poor fellow sighing that his right arm was shattered beyond hope of striking another blow for freedom![80]

The routine nature of hospital work was also disrupted by various medical emergencies. A frequent problem was secondary hemorrhage in which an amputation or other wound that was healing began bleeding again. Union contract surgeon David Warman was roused from his bed late one night when a soldier who had been shot in the leg began to hemorrhage. In his diary, Warman explained the medical problem: "Secondary hemorrhage had resulted at three different times. We decided that the only chance for life was amputation which was accordingly done, and the life saved. These minnie' [sic] balls make an ugly wound."[81]

STEWARDS AND NURSES

Although doctors were needed for such major emergencies, every hospital had scores of other staff members who could handle minor medical matters. The main helpers doctors had were medical stewards and nurses. Stewards were male soldiers who knew a lot about medicine and worked closely with doctors. Hospitals usually had one steward for every one hundred patients. Stewards cleaned and bandaged wounds, monitored the medical progress of patients, and distributed medicine. However, because both the Union and the Confederacy needed every soldier, both sides began hiring women to serve as nurses and to supplement the dwindling supply of stewards.

It was unusual in this period for women to work outside the home, but Florence Nightingale and her small band of English nurses had done such

a good job of caring for soldiers during the Crimean War in Europe from 1854 to 1856 that it had become acceptable for women to enter this profession. During the Civil War, the standard hospital ratio was eleven nurses for every one hundred patients. Because nurses in this period had little medical training, they performed mostly menial jobs such as serving meals, changing bedding, and assisting doctors on their daily rounds. They also did things to comfort patients, including writing letters for illiterate soldiers.

While the army had always had medical stewards, and doctors had no trouble working with them, many physicians opposed the induction of female nurses. The naysayers argued that women lacked medical knowledge and that it was improper for women to work around so many men. One Confederate medical director claimed his hospital had "miserable nurses [who] did not know castor oil from a gun rod nor laudanum [a painkiller] from a hole in the ground."[82] Some doctors, however, appreciated the tireless efforts of many female nurses. Union surgeon Alfred Lewis Castleman, for example, was so worried that nurses in his hospital were working too hard and that they might become sick that he began to do some of their chores. Castleman wrote in 1863, "I, after my official duties of the day were over, did, for weeks together, spend the greater

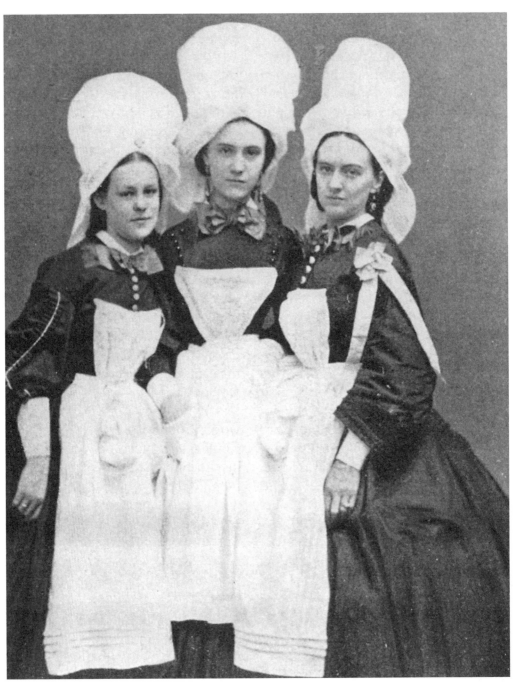

A fund-raising photo depicts ideally attired nurses from the Civil War era. In reality, nurses wore slightly less elaborate dress to help them perform their duties with greater ease.

part of every night in the unofficial, and, perhaps, undignified capacity of nurse, sending the exhausted nurses to their beds and ministering to the wants of the sick. I rarely retired before two o'clock in the morning."[83]

In addition to becoming exhausted, many nurses did become sick from tending patients. One was Louisa May Alcott, who later became famous for writing *Little Women* and other novels. While working at Union Hospital in Washington, Alcott contracted typhoid fever and almost died.

THE WOUND DRESSER

Another famous literary figure who worked in hospitals was poet Walt Whitman. In December 1862, after visiting his brother, George, who had been injured in the Battle of Fredericksburg, Whitman became interested in trying to boost the morale of other sick and wounded soldiers. Whitman estimated that in three years he made more than six hundred visits to hospitals and battlefields and met almost one hundred thousand soldiers.

Whitman was only one of thousands of men and women who spent

Soldiers and medical staff members pose outside Campbell Hospital in Washington, D.C. Campbell was one of many permanent convalescent facilities built for the Union Army.

✎ MAKING SOLDIERS CHEERFUL ↬

Union surgeon Alfred Lewis Castleman was ahead of his time in realizing that relieving depression in sick and wounded patients could help them get well. In 1863 Castleman wrote about his experiences in The Army of the Potomac: Behind the Scenes, *his Civil War memoir. Castleman claimed that making patients happy was important to their recovery, and he detailed how he tried to cheer up patients:*

I think my hospital can boast, just now, the happiest set of sick men I ever saw. This morning, as I was prescribing for them (all sitting up) some were reading the morning papers and talking loudly over war news, some playing [cards], some checkers, some chess, some dominoes—all laughing and merry. [There] is no disease so contagious, or so depressing to vital energy, as inactivity and gloominess of mind. Introduce one such temperament into your hospital, *without an accompanying antidote*, and the condition will be communicated to all others in the hospital, with as much certainty, and with greater rapidity, than would the infection of small-pox or measles. I recommend that the Surgeon pass frequently through his hospital, making it a rule never to leave till he has elicited a hearty laugh from every one in it. [And the doctor should] introduce light reading, chess-men, checkers, dominoes, cards, puzzles, their use to be regulated by a corps of jolly, mirth loving, but judicious nurses.

time cheering up soldiers, and in his book *Memoranda During the War*, he described the results of his efforts. Whitman performed a few minor medical duties, such as changing dirty bandages, but he spent most of his time talking to soldiers, playing games with them such as checkers, and distributing books, tobacco, and other small gifts. Whitman said of his hospital visits, "I found it was in the simple matter of personal presence and emanating ordinary cheer and magnetism that I succeeded and helped more than by medical nursing."[84]

Whitman's chronicle of his volunteer work in *Memoranda* and poems such as "The Wound Dresser" also provide some of the most dramatic descriptions ever written of Civil War hospitals. His eye for detail is evident in this passage about a ward in Campbell Hospital in Washington:

It contains to-day, I should judge, eighty or a hundred patients, half sick, half wounded. You walk down the central passage, with a row on either side, their feet toward you, and their heads to the wall. You may hear groans, or other sounds of unendurable suffering, from two or three of the iron cots, but in the main there is quiet—almost a painful absence of demonstration; but the pallid face, the dull'd eye, and the moisture on the lip, are demonstration enough.[85]

DANGER FOR DOCTORS

Thousands of Confederate and Union doctors were part of hospital scenes such as Whitman described. But even though they worked far from the field of battle, their lives were sometimes in danger. When Union assistant surgeon John G. Perry arrived at Chesapeake Hospital in May 1862, he was warned to be careful when treating Confederate prisoners of war. Perry recalled, "I [was told] that the surgeon who served before me, while dressing a soldier's wound, laid the knife down for a moment on the bed. The man seized it and made a lunge at the doctor, but instead of killing him, as he had intended, only ran it into his arm; whereupon the doctor instantly shot him."[86] The danger that existed even in hospitals where the only duty was to help patients—even enemy soldiers—only proved how terrible the war could be.

CHAPTER 5

FIGHTING DISEASE, THE CIVIL WAR'S PRIME KILLER

In April 1862 Union contract surgeon John Vance Lauderdale was working aboard the *D.A. January*, a paddle-wheel hospital ship churning its way up the Tennessee River to St. Louis, Missouri, with sick and wounded soldiers from the Battle of Shiloh. Although shocked by the combat injuries, Lauderdale was even more horrified by the devastating diseases that were killing soldiers as surely as bullets from enemy guns. In his diary entry for April 29, Lauderdale commented:

> There are several very sick men—their disease is typhoid fever. We lost one this morning, and we fear many will go off [die] before morning. Our treatment of these cases is very unsatisfactory, because we do not see them 'till the disease has nearly destroyed them. I would almost as soon die in battle as to fall a victim to fever.[87]

Of the estimated 620,000 Union and Confederate soldiers who lost their lives in the Civil War, 2 out of every 3 died from disease rather than battle wounds. Union doctors treated some 7 million cases of disease-related illness, and the Confederates contended with several million more. Outbreaks of contagious diseases such as measles, smallpox, and malaria repeatedly struck both armies. Filthy conditions that bred illnesses like diarrhea and typhoid fever sickened and killed tens of thousands of soldiers. A lack of cleanliness by doctors themselves led to postsurgery infections that killed thousands of soldiers who would have recovered from their wounds.

Although such diseases are rarely fatal today, they were during the war because doctors did not know what caused them or how to treat them. In fact, the war's first great wave of ill-

This camp on the outskirts of Petersburg, Virginia, was abandoned by its Confederate defenders. It was then captured by the Union Army and turned into a field hospital.

ness killed thousands of soldiers before they had a chance to fight.

CONTAGIOUS DISEASES

In the opening months of the conflict, Union and Confederate recruits began training to become soldiers. Not long after their arrival in military camps, thousands of them became ill with measles. Confederate surgeon Archibald Atkinson Jr. described in his diary how widespread the disease

was: "There was an epidemic of measles in the army [and] every soldier who had not been 10 miles from his home before he enlisted was seized with it. I've had boys of 16, [and] fathers of 60 years lying side by side on straw beds placed on the floor all suffering from measles or some of its complications."[88]

Measles is a contagious disease, one that is easily transmitted from person to person. It spread quickly in training camps because most recruits were from isolated rural areas and had never been exposed to the measles virus, the microscopic living organism that caused the disease. Measles is not usually fatal to children, but the symptoms are much more severe in adults. During the war, the high fevers and other symptoms of measles killed 4,246 Union soldiers and an unknown number of Confederates.

During the war, several other contagious diseases, including smallpox, swept through military camps with such frequency that doctors collectively called them camp fevers. Although doctors thought such diseases were caused by miasms rather than by viruses, they did know that they were contagious. In a Civil War medical manual that he wrote, Confederate surgeon J. Julian Chisolm advised doctors that "[fever] cases should, if possible, be isolated in tents, and ample room be given to each."[89] Doctors on both sides agreed with Chisolm and routinely segregated patients in camps and hospitals.

FILTHY CONDITIONS

Diseases carried by viruses killed thousands of soldiers. However, many of the war's worst diseases had a different cause—the dirt and filth in which soldiers lived. When Union surgeon general William A. Hammond visited a camp in Virginia in March 1862, he was appalled by trash and dirt in the soldiers' living area. He noted, "The tents are in a very bad state of police [a military term for cleanliness]. The effluvia [smell] from them, on entering, was stifling."[90] After a similar inspection of camps near Washington, D.C., a civilian group that worked to improve the health of soldiers also criticized filthy conditions. The U.S. Sanitary Commission said the most serious problem was the sinks, the military name for outdoor toilets: "In most cases the only sink is merely a straight trench, some thirty feet long unprovided with a pole or rail [to support soldiers]; the edges are filthy, and the stench exceedingly offensive. . . . [Some are so foul] that the men avoid use of the sinks [and relieve themselves] wherever convenient."[91]

Although doctors then did not know it, the decomposing garbage, spoiled food, and human waste that littered military camps and the tents soldiers slept in were breeding grounds for bacteria, microscopic living organisms that cause diseases such as typhoid fever, diarrhea, and cholera. Soldiers became ill by coming into physical contact with bacteria or by eating and drinking contaminated food or water.

Camp sinks were a major source of illness because they were often placed so close to rivers and lakes that human waste leaked into the water sources. After tens of thousands of soldiers in 1862 had spent weeks along the Tennessee River during the Battle of Shiloh, a *Chicago Tribune* newspaper reporter wrote that the river "smells so offensive that the men had to hold their noses while drinking it."[92] The foul smell meant the water was contaminated with waste. When soldiers gulped it because there was nothing else to drink, some became sick with diseases such as typhoid fever.

Union records show that 27,056 soldiers died from typhoid fever, a noncontagious disease that also killed many Confederates. But the war's most common and deadly disease was chronic diarrhea, an illness some doctors also labeled dysentery. There were many causes for diarrhea, including water contamination, spoiled food, and a poor diet. Union records show that nearly 1.6 million soldiers had this disease. Of those, 27,558 of them died of the disease, and 16,183 received medical discharges because it permanently disabled them. The

In October 1862 the Union Army occupied the partially destroyed town of Harper's Ferry, Virginia. Situated among the rubble, the Union camps were breeding grounds for disease.

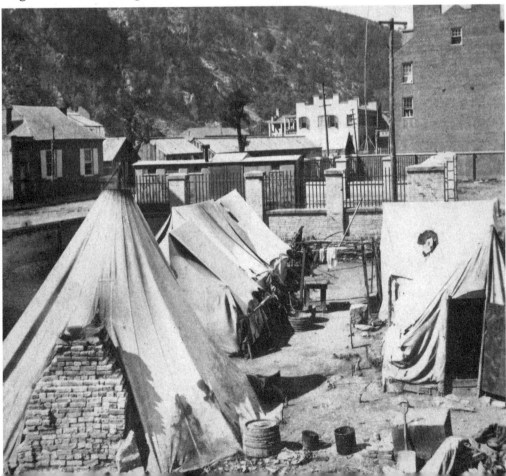

disease was believed to have been even more widespread among Confederates, who jokingly gave it the military title "General Diarrhea" because nearly every soldier suffered from it. Even doctors were not immune from it. In his diary for July 2, 1862, Union assistant surgeon Cyrus Bacon Jr. wrote, "Am still required to be abed [in bed] most of the time. There is so much prostration in this diarrhea that it is with much difficulty I force my mind to anything."[93]

Soldiers tolerated filthy conditions because they did not understand the link between dirt and disease and because people during this era generally had a lower standard of personal cleanliness than people have today. For example, many soldiers did not bathe or change their clothes for weeks at a time. This general disregard for cleanliness created another family of war diseases—wound infections.

WOUNDS BECOME INFECTED

When soldiers were struck by a minié ball or cut by a saber, their lives were endangered in two ways: first, by phys-

---

♪ FILTHY SURGEONS ♫

W.W. Keen wrote an article in 1905 about his experiences as a Union surgeon. Keen explained that Civil War doctors who operated in filthy clothes and with unwashed medical instruments did not know they could infect their patients. Keen's vivid description of the dirty conditions he labored in has been reprinted on the Web site of the Society of Civil War Surgeons:

We operated in old blood-stained and often pus-stained coats, the veterans of a hundred fights. We used undisinfected instruments from undisinfected plush-lined cases, and still worse, used marine sponges which had been used in prior pus cases and had been only washed in tap water. If a sponge or an instrument fell on the floor it was washed and squeezed in a basin of tap water and used as if it were clean. Our silk to tie blood vessels was undisinfected. The silk with which we sewed up all wounds was undisinfected. If there was any difficulty in threading the needle we moistened it with bacteria laden saliva [from their mouths], and rolled it between bacteria-infected fingers. We dressed the wounds with clean but undisinfected sheets, shirts, tablecloths, or other old soft linen rescued from the family ragbag [of the house they were using]. We had no sterilized gauze dressing, no gauze sponges. We knew nothing about antiseptics [chemicals that kill bacteria] and therefore used none.

ical damage from the weapon, and second, by bacteria that could enter the wound and create deadly infections. Bacteria were carried into wounds in many ways—on the bullets or blades themselves, on bits of debris driven into the body by the force of the injuring blow, or on dirt and filth that touched the wound while the soldier was waiting to be treated.

Even in the hospital, soldiers were not safe from infection. The cruelest irony concerning the doctors' ignorance about disease was that they infected many of their patients by allowing themselves, their instruments, and their operating rooms to be dirty and thus full of bacteria. Union surgeon Edward L. Munson commented on this years after the war ended:

The cleanliness of wounds was regarded as of little or no importance. Under the surgical practice of the time, germs were almost always conveyed into the body [by doctors]. It was the custom for the surgeons to [operate under] conditions in which even a pretense of surgical cleanliness [was] not maintained.[94]

Because doctors did not know bacteria from dirty conditions caused infection, they accidentally spread illness from patient to patient. They did this by poking and prodding one wound after another for hours without washing their bloody hands and by using the same surgical instruments over and over without cleaning them. The white coats they wore became covered with blood, human tissue, and dirt. The floors of their operating rooms became wet with blood and littered with soiled bandages, dirty clothing cut from wounded soldiers, and amputated limbs.

Surgery performed under such conditions is called septic because it allows bacteria to infect patients; it is the opposite of antiseptic surgery, in which operating rooms are kept free of bacteria. Because of septic conditions, wound infection was so universal that doctors believed it was part of the natural healing process. Thus, they were never alarmed when a wound became red and inflamed and began leaking thick yellow pus, symptoms physicians today recognize as dangerous signs of infection. Civil War doctors even called the wound discharge "laudable pus" because they believed its presence meant the wound was healing and thus should be lauded, or praised.

DEADLY INFECTIONS

Although the early symptoms of all infections were those that doctors believed showed wounds were healing, they recognized later symptoms that indicated their patients had a life-threatening infection. Union surgeon W.W. Keen explained:

Many a time have I had the following experience: A poor fellow whose leg or arm I had amputated a few days before would be getting on as well as we then expected—that is to say, he had pain, high fever, was thirsty and restless, but was gradually improving, for he had what we looked on as a favorable symptom—an abundant discharge of pus from his wound. Suddenly, overnight, I would find that his fever had become markedly greater; his tongue dry, his pain and restlessness increased [and] the secretions from the wound almost dried up.[95]

The new symptoms indicated the patient had one of several deadly infections. The most serious were gan-

A doctor performs an amputation in the squalid conditions of a makeshift operating room. Because field hospitals were not sterile environments, surgery often left patients with infected wounds.

grene, which destroys tissue; pyemia, which enters the blood system and spreads throughout the body to damage the heart and other organs; and tetanus, which causes painful muscular rigidity and muscular contractions that can lead to death. Gangrene was perhaps the most horrifying since it turns healthy skin and tissue black and gradually begins eating away at them to expose bones and arteries. Union surgeon Silas Weir Mitchell described how quickly gangrene could damage a patient: "A slight flesh wound began to show a gray edge of slough [dying skin], and within two hours we saw this widening at the rate of half an inch an hour, and deepening."[96]

FAILED TREATMENTS

The reason so many soldiers with infections died is because doctors did not know how to cure them. In a letter to his wife, Union assistant surgeon Cyrus Bacon Jr. wrote, "I am sorry the men suffer so from pyemia. It is almost surely fatal and nearly all the ball wounds terminate in it, or in gangrene."[97] Pyemia, known today as blood poisoning, was fatal to 2,747 of 2,812 Union soldiers who contracted the disease. Gangrene was the next most fatal, killing 45 percent of Union soldiers with the infection.

Confederate soldiers suffered equally from such infections despite the efforts of doctors to treat a sickness they did not understand. In a medical manual he wrote for Confederate doctors, Surgeon Edward Warren suggested the following treatment for soldiers with the deadliest wound infection: "Pyemia requires to be treated by tonics, stimulants, and a nutritious diet. The restlessness and insomnia [of the patient] must be controlled with opium; the diarrhea with opium and astringents combined to help blood clot."[98]

Although the measures might have alleviated some of the patient's symptoms, they could not kill an infection caused by bacteria. Doctors were just as helpless in treating gangrene. When this and other infections appeared, the only hope doctors had of saving the patient was to amputate the limb above the infected spot, thus ridding the body of the infection. Doctors sometimes had to perform several amputations to halt the infection's spread, with each operation leaving the patient with an ever-shorter arm or leg.

Because their treatments did nothing to cure the illness, doctors had a similar lack of success in combating many other diseases. For example, doctors gave typhoid fever patients drugs to make them vomit and used one of several methods to bleed them. Both techniques were supposed to allow the illness to leave the patient's body, but all they did was further weaken a patient who was already sick with fever and diarrhea.

🔥 MALARIA STRIKES 🔥

Malaria was one of the Civil War's most common diseases. Although malaria's alternating attacks of chills and high fevers can be fatal, quinine was able to stop the symptoms and save lives. In this excerpt from Robert E. Denney's Civil War Medicine: Care & Comfort of the Wounded, *Union surgeon George E. Cooper explains how a wave of malaria struck soldiers in his care in November 1861 at Hilton Head, South Carolina:*

Shortly after the troops were disembarked [from ships], the malarious fevers of the southern coast began to show themselves. The fevers by which the men were attacked shortly after their arrival were, in many cases, of the most malignant type, and in some cases the [ill soldiers] sank on the first chill. Men were brought into the hospital with what would be regarded as epileptic fits, but what, in reality, was the coast fever. These would froth at the mouth, have some convulsions, and, for a time, be perfectly demented. The chief complaints made by them were of severe headache, and of a burning skin, when in reality the surface was cold and covered with a clammy sweat. [Later] the skin became excessively hot, the eyes bloodshot, the pulse [very fast]. When the fever broke up the heavy sweat was of a most disagreeable odor. The only hope for the patient was doses of quinine.

Most of the drugs doctors prescribed were ineffective, and some were even dangerous to their patients. For example, doctors gave typhoid fever patients calomel, one of the war's most commonly prescribed drugs. But calomel's main ingredient—mercury—is poisonous in high doses, and some patients became sick or died from receiving too much of it. One such victim was author Louisa May Alcott, who lost most of her hair and teeth to calomel when she was treated for typhoid fever while working as a nurse. In May 1863 Union surgeon general Hammond became so concerned about calomel and tartar emetic, another mercury-based drug, that he ordered doctors to quit using them. In issuing his order, Hammond claimed, "[These drugs are used] indiscriminately and excessively, thereby causing the loss of teeth, and sometimes mercurial [poisoning], resulting in the rotting of the soft parts of the mouth and cheeks, which were expelled [by patients] as a putrid mass."[99] Hammond's ban did not last long, though. He was removed from office a few months later due to an unrelated matter, leaving doctors free to resume prescribing the suspect drug for a wide range of diseases.

SUCCESSES BATTLING DISEASE

Civil War doctors, however, were not helpless against all illness. They were successful in fighting several diseases because they had effective drugs and treatments.

Malaria is transmitted by mosquitoes infected with the malaria virus. Although 1 million Union soldiers had malaria, only 5,000 died of the disease. This was because malaria was treatable. Doctors on both sides saved lives by administering quinine, a drug that could stop malaria's deadly fevers and chills. During a malaria outbreak in August 1864, Confederate surgeon Herbert M. Nash theorized that the disease was also killing horses, which were desperately needed to pull heavy artillery pieces. Nash dosed the horses with quinine and was overjoyed with the result: "I [gave it] to each horse as soon as the symptoms appeared. I am glad to relate that not another horse died."[100]

Smallpox was another contagious disease that killed several thousand soldiers during the war. There were no drugs to treat smallpox, but it

A wagon acts as a field pharmacy where doctors dispensed drugs to those in need. Because drugs were always in short supply, soldiers on both sides prized the capture of enemy medical wagons.

could be prevented through vaccination. Although doctors on both sides greatly reduced the number of victims by vaccinating soldiers, the vaccinations were not always effective. Some of the smartest doctors, however, learned how to successfully protect their men against the disease. Union surgeon Albert Gaillard Hart claimed he kept soldiers in his Ohio regiment healthy by vaccinating them several times instead of just once. Boasted Hart, "The result was complete immunity from smallpox on the part of the regiment [while] regiments around us, not revaccinated, suffered severely from the disease."[101]

One of the best methods doctors discovered to fight illness was to issue orders to clean up camps. Although they did not understand that it was bacteria from filthy conditions that caused disease, many knew from personal experience that improved sanitation reduced illness. As more doctors learned this lesson during the war, the high rate of diseases such as diarrhea and typhoid fever began to decline. When Union surgeon Alfred Lewis Castleman arrived at Camp Curtin in Harrisburg, Pennsylvania, in 1863, he said "the stench of the camp was intolerable, and the sickness of the troops rapidly increased."[102] His remedy was to order soldiers to clear away garbage, wash themselves and their clothes, and regularly cover sinks with layers of dirt. Castleman said he

noticed a difference within a short time: "The result has been most striking. The sick list has already, in only six days, decreased fifty in number."[103]

SCURVY AND PNEUMONIA

Many diseases that struck soldiers were unrelated to contagion or filthy conditions. Two of the most widespread were scurvy and pneumonia.

Scurvy, which Civil War doctors referred to by the old-fashioned term *scorbutus*, is caused by a lack of vitamin C. This deficiency makes people tired, listless, and susceptible to other illnesses. It also causes mouth ulcers that make their teeth fall out. Scurvy was a serious problem during the war because it not only endangered the health of soldiers but also their effectiveness as a fighting force. In early 1863, when many Confederate soldiers began developing scurvy, Surgeon Lafayette Guild claimed that unless the army gave its men more vegetables they would become so weak that "our next [military] campaign may be a disastrous one, simply for the want of an antiscorbutics."[104]

As Guild noted, the cure for scurvy is the vitamins provided by fresh fruits and vegetables. Both sides, however, often found it difficult to supply soldiers with those food items. When that happened, doctors had soldiers gather wild onions and other available plants and add them to soups and

❧ NATURAL DRUGS ❧

During the Civil War, Union ships blocked shipments of medical drugs to Southern ports. When Confederate doctors ran short of drugs, many had no choice but to turn to old-fashioned home remedies made from plants and trees. The following narrative, from the Civil War Home Internet site, reveals how one unnamed doctor used natural remedies when supplies ran low.

I perused my dispensary and called into requisition an old botanic practice [book] which had been handed down as a relic of the past, but from which I confess to have received valuable aid and very many useful hints in regard to the medical virtues of our native plants. In stomach and bowel diseases I found but little difficulty in obtaining plenty of substitutes for [drugs]; in fact, I believe that an all wise Providence has especially provided the best antidotes in creation on the hills and dales, and by the vales and streams of our own Southland. In ordinary loose-ness of the bowels or diarrhea, I gave an infusion of raspberry leaves or whortleberry leaves (both of which act finely on the kidneys and bladder). Where there was nausea or sick stomach, a handful of peach leaves steeped in water and drank will settle it, or what is perhaps better, the kernel of two or three [peach] seeds cracked and cold water drank off of them. If stronger [medicine] is necessary, the inner bark of red oak, blackberry or dewberry root tea, or red shank root, are sure remedies.

stews they ate. In addition, civilian groups and private individuals on both sides often brought fruit and vegetables to nearby camps. When Union surgeon John S. Billings was in charge of Cliffburne Hospital in Washington, D.C., a congressman asked him what he could do for sick and wounded soldiers from his state. "They have all got more or less scurvy," Billings told the legislator, "and I think fresh strawberries would do them good."[105] The congressman purchased strawberries and other fruits, and the patients became healthier.

There was no simple cure, however, for one of the war's worst diseases—pneumonia. Only diarrhea and typhoid fever killed more men than this respiratory disease, which took the lives of twenty thousand Union soldiers and an untold number of Confederates. Pneumonia was caused by exposure to wet and cold conditions such as those that Union surgeon John Alexander Ritter described in a February 28, 1862, letter. Ritter told his wife that after he and the men in his regiment became soaked and chilled by a rainstorm at Camp

Cumberland in Kentucky, many of them became sick. "All of our clothing [and other belongings were] wet," Ritter explained. "It was altogether the hardest time that I have seen since I have been in the service. It was enough to kill a grown hog and from the effects a number of men are not so well."[106] Ritter added that a soldier named Bent McColley was very sick and would probably die despite his best efforts to save him. "You may informe [*sic*] his people,"[107] the doctor wrote, knowing the family would want to know about their son's imminent death.

NOTHING THEY COULD DO

Even though Civil War doctors dealt daily with wounds and diseases that defied their skill to cure, they were still saddened by death. Such feelings were summed up in a diary entry Union contract surgeon David Warman wrote in August 1864 after two patients died:

> Ramson and Morrill both died today. The death of Morrill [from tetanus] was most pathetic. He was conscious to the last. And thus it goes on. Every day, the brightest and best of our young men are cut down in the flower of their young manhood and placed in untimely graves. How long, Oh Lord, how long is this state of things going to last before we have peace?[108]

CHAPTER 6

CIVIL WAR INNOVATIONS IN MEDICAL CARE

On May 21, 1862, Union surgeon general William A. Hammond established the Army Medical Museum to collect and preserve historical items that would illustrate for future generations how Civil War surgeons had treated ill and wounded soldiers. Hammond ordered medical officers to contribute reports on interesting cases along with physical specimens such as amputated leg bones and diseased organs preserved in chemicals. Although some citizens later complained the collection was ghoulish, Union surgeon John Hill Brinton defended it. Brinton, the museum's first curator, said, "[The museum was founded] not for the collection of curiosities, but for the accumulation of objects and data of lasting scientific significance, which might in the future serve to instruct generations of students, and thus in time be productive of real use."[109]

In addition to becoming an important resource to educate future military doctors, the Washington, D.C., museum, today known as the National Museum of Health and Medicine, also bears witness today to the many medical advancements that were made during the Civil War. Union and Confederate doctors perfected the use of anesthetics—chloroform and ether—to spare wounded soldiers the agony of surgery. Their ingenuity and willingness to try innovative procedures to help patients resulted in new surgical techniques, including facial reconstruction through plastic surgery. Their efforts to help soldiers deal with continuing pain from war wounds laid the foundation for the establishment of neurology, a new branch of medical study on how the nervous system affects the body. Decades before development of theories on human psychology, doctors even helped soldiers deal with problems that today are considered forms of mental illness.

BLESSED PAINKILLERS

The physical devastation the war caused provided doctors a working laboratory to research new medical treatments. One of the most beneficial was use of anesthetics, drugs that rendered patients unconscious.

Before Confederate surgeon Hunter Holmes McGuire amputated the left

Many battlefield surgeries were performed with the aid of sleep-inducing drugs. This one-pound can held ether, an efficient but very flammable anesthetic.

arm of General Thomas "Stonewall" Jackson, he put Jackson to sleep with chloroform. McGuire later described how Jackson, who had several painful wounds, reacted to the drug: "As he began to feel its effects, and its relief to the pain he was suffering, he exclaimed 'What an infinite blessing,' and continued to repeat the word 'blessing' until he became insensible."[110]

Ether and chloroform, which render people unconscious, were first introduced to America in the late 1840s. For more than a decade, however, most doctors feared to use anesthetics because their inexperience in administering them killed many patients. The same fear kept some British doctors from giving anesthesia to wounded soldiers during the Crimean War, which ended in 1856. But during the Civil War, American doctors learned to rely on anesthetics to perform amputations and other painful medical procedures.

Union doctors gave patients anesthetics at least eighty thousand times, and Confederate doctors also used them extensively. The Battle of Iuka in Mississippi on September 19, 1862, was the only large fight in which either side failed to employ anesthetics when they were available. Confederate surgeon A.B. Campbell, medical director of the Army of the Mississippi, reported, "No anesthetics were used, and [ironically] not a groan or sign of pain was heard."[111] It is not known why doctors decided not to use them, but Iuka proved to be the exception.

When the war began, the most common method of administering ether or chloroform was to wet a cloth or sponge with the drug and hold it over a patient's nose. But Confederate doctor J. Julian Chisolm invented an inhaler that channeled the drug directly to the patient's nostrils. This cut down on the amount needed to put the injured person to sleep. Physicians on both sides began using funnels or cones as inhalers similar to Chisolm's invention. Doctors came to prefer chloroform, partly because ether was flammable. In a speech years later, Union surgeon W.W. Keen remembered a near tragedy when candle flames ignited ether fumes while he was performing a nighttime operation. Keen recalled, "I have often wondered why I did not have the sense to use chloroform. Suddenly the ether [located near the candles] took fire and the etherizer [his assistant] flung away both cone and bottle. Luckily the bottle did not break or we might have had an ugly fire in a hospital constructed wholly of wood."[112]

Only forty-three Union soldiers given anesthetics died from them. One reason for this remarkably low death rate was that doctors used only enough to make patients lightly unconscious. An unfortunate side effect of this judicious use of anesthesia was that soldiers often groaned or thrashed about during surgery even though they did not consciously feel pain. People who witnessed this believed doctors had not used any anesthetic. The accounts these observers wrote led many future historians to falsely believe the same thing.

Anesthetics allowed Civil War doctors to perform longer, more complex operations. That became an important factor in helping them develop new surgical techniques.

PLASTIC SURGERY

Between 1870 and 1888 the Army Medical Museum published the six volumes of the *Medical and Surgical History of the War of the Rebellion*, a six-thousand-page study that documents the medical histories of tens of thousands of sick and injured Union and Confederate soldiers. Among hundreds of photographs of unusual injuries are before and after pictures of Private Carleton Burgan, whose disfigured face was surgically reconstructed in one of the first documented cases of plastic surgery.

Burgan was one of thirty-two Union soldiers who had their faces partially rebuilt through operations that can be considered plastic surgery. The term

---

ꙮ UNCOVERING MALINGERERS ꙮ

When Union surgeon W.W. Keen was working at Turner's Lane Hospital in Philadelphia, he learned an interesting new use for anesthetics. Malingerers were soldiers who faked injuries such as blindness so they would not have to fight. Keen and other doctors discovered they could trick malingerers who were healthy by giving them ether to make them unconscious and then testing their reactions when the soldiers woke up. In this excerpt from his memoirs, posted on the Web site of the Society of Civil War Surgeons, Keen explains how this worked:

[Ether] proved a most efficient method of detection. For instance, in asserted blindness we suggested that the man should be etherized, the sound eye then covered with adhesive plaster, and, when recovering from the anaesthetic, before he was able to reason and guard himself against making mistakes, that his sight should be tested by very simple means, such as holding out to him in the hand some water or some whiskey, or any other act which would reveal the presence or absence of sight in the supposed blind eye. Hearing can [also] be tested during the recovery stage of ether when the patient is taken unawares [and] in one of our cases aphonia [inability to speak] was detected without the slightest difficulty. The patient, however, quickly recovered himself and fell at the surgeon's feet with clasped hands, exclaiming with a voice and attitude worthy of [an actor]: "Thank God, Doctor, you have restored my voice!"

---

plastic comes from the Greek word *plastikos*, which means "to mold or give form." The delicate operations to sew together soft tissues of the eyelids, nose, and mouth and to restore the shape provided by missing facial bones would not have been possible without anesthesia to keep the patients unconscious for a long period.

Although most soldiers who had such surgery were victims of battle wounds, Burgan's face was disfigured in August 1863 after he was given too much calomel while hospitalized for pneumonia. The mercury created a gangrenous ulcer that destroyed his upper mouth, palate, right cheek, and right eye and forced doctors to remove his right cheek bone. Gurdon Buck, a civilian physician, rebuilt Burgan's face with a series of operations and dental and facial implants that replaced missing teeth and bone. Buck similarly helped many disfigured soldiers and is considered a pioneer in plastic surgery.

Buck's surgery reduced the physical signs of facial damage so much that Burgan was able to lead a normal life. Other innovations in surgery, however, actually saved the lives of soldiers.

BRAIN SURGERY

Although most Civil War doctors had never treated a brain injury, they learned or invented new techniques to handle the serious head wounds produced by the fighting. One procedure was trephination, in which doctors drilled a circular hole into the skull to relieve cranial pressure or to remove metal or bone fragments pressing on the brain. In 1862, when Corporal Edson D. Bemis was struck in the head by a minié ball, Union surgeon

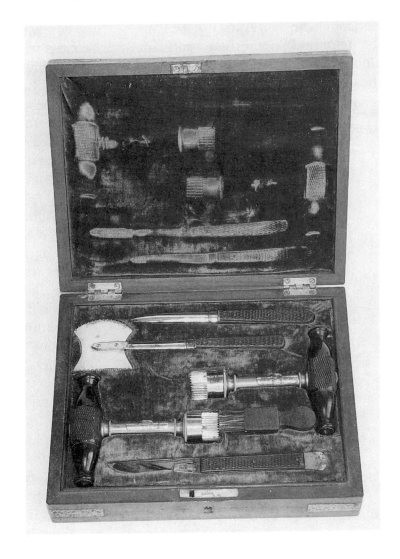

A brain surgeon's trephination kit contained knives to flense away cranial skin and t-shaped borers to drill into the skull cavity.

A. Vandermeer used trephination to widen the hole the ball had made. He then pulled the bullet out with a metal probe. Bemis recovered, and in 1870 he wrote to army doctors to inform them that "I am still in the land of the living [but] my head aches some of the time."[113]

The war's most famous head-wound patient was President Abraham Lincoln, who died April 15, 1865, after actor and Southern sympathizer John Wilkes Booth shot him in the head five days after the war ended.

General Joseph Barnes was one of the doctors that tended to President Abraham Lincoln after he was shot on April 14, 1865.

The *Medical and Surgical History of the War of the Rebellion* includes this description of the treatment Lincoln received:

After the administration of a small quantity of brandy and water the patient was removed [from Ford's Theatre] to a neighboring house. His clothing was removed, and he was placed in bed. His extremities were cold. He was covered with warmed blankets, and bottles of hot water were applied to the lower extremities. . . . The protracted death-struggle ceased at twenty minutes past seven o'clock on the morning of April 15th, 1865.[114]

Although Lincoln was cared for by Surgeon General Joseph K. Barnes and other fine doctors, their lack of skill in treating head wounds prevented them from removing the bullet or doing anything significant to save his life. The same inexperience in performing operations involving the head and brain led to the deaths of over half the 221 Union soldiers who had trephinations. In addition, the poking and prodding doctors did in trying to save the lives of head-wound victims often destroyed parts of their brains, thus impairing their ability to speak, remember things, or perform other mental tasks.

Doctors who performed brain surgery were also handicapped by a lack of proper instruments designed to do such delicate procedures. Confederate surgeon Hunter Holmes McGuire explained that this forced doctors to be creative when doing such surgery: "I have seen [a doctor] break off one prong of a common table-fork, bend the point of the other prong, and with it elevate the bone in [a case of] depressed fracture of the skull and save life."[115]

In addition to using their ingenuity to fashion instruments, many doctors created new techniques to treat wounds or illness. Some of these experiments proved fortuitous and saved many lives.

OTHER MEDICAL ADVANCEMENTS

Early in the war, soldiers with serious chest wounds almost always died. The reason was that when the chest wall was punctured, pressure in the chest dropped and one or both lungs collapsed. When that happened, soldiers could not breathe and quickly suffocated. But on June 25, 1863, Assistant Surgeon Benjamin Howard asked the Union army to test a procedure he had perfected that could seal a chest wound to prevent that from happening. His method to close the wound included metal sutures and

several layers of bandages soaked in collodion, a chemical that, as it dried, stiffened the cloth to create a firm seal. Many soldiers still died, either because of a lack of expertise in sealing the wound or infections that almost always occurred in such injuries.

Howard's method became standard treatment for what doctors called "sucking chest wounds," a name that came from the noise of escaping air. Union surgeon John S. Billings praised Howard's method because it helped soldiers keep breathing: "The immediate relief it affords is marked; quiet, tranquil respiration follows."[116] Confederate doctors saved many lives by using similar methods after they learned of Howard's discovery.

James Baxter Bean, a Confederate dentist, was responsible for another innovation in treating injuries—the interdental splint for broken jaws. Before Bean, doctors treated this injury with a splint that kept the broken bones immobile, which often resulted in deformities in the healed jaw that made patients look disfigured and also impaired their ability to speak and eat. Bean's splint eliminated such problems by keeping teeth in proper alignment so the jaw could heal correctly. The splint had rubber to make it flexible, and that made it easier for the patient to eat and talk while the jaw was healing. When Bean gave Confederate surgeon Samuel H. Stout a tour of his "broken jaw ward," the high-ranking medical officer said he was amazed to be greeted with "great hilarity by the patients, who were able to converse freely and distinctly with me."[117]

Although Bean developed the new splint based on knowledge he had of

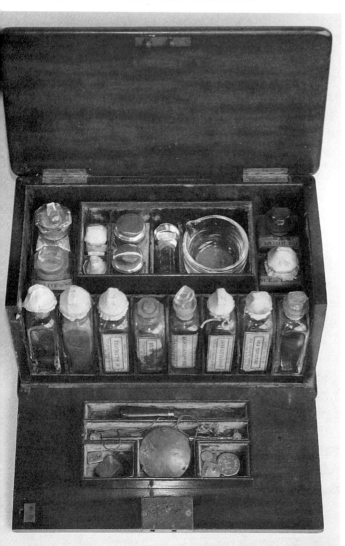

A well-stocked Civil War medical chest contained various elixirs used to ward off infection. Some of these agents were traditional concoctions, while others like bromine were novel chemical treatments.

human anatomy, some doctors accidentally stumbled on wartime innovations while experimenting. One of the most important discoveries was by Union surgeon Middleton Goldsmith, who found a way to cure infections even though he was unaware that bacteria caused them. In an effort to stop infections, he applied various chemicals to infected wounds to see if any would work. When he doused an infected wound with bromine, a chemical that kills bacteria, he found his magic elixir.

The use of bacteria-killing substances such as bromine did not become widespread until several years after the war, when scientists discovered the relationship between bacteria and infection. But when Goldsmith's findings became public midway through the war, a few doctors on both sides began using bromine even though they did not know why it worked. Years later, after the true cause of infection had been revealed, Union surgeon W.W. Keen wrote of bromine: "Our method of treating gangrene, which was empirical [by experimenting], we now know to have been based on sound [scientific] grounds."[118]

One of the strangest medical discoveries involved the use of maggots, the insect larvae that appeared in almost every wound because insects were drawn to the warm tissue as a haven to lay their eggs. Although the maggots did not cause any pain, medical personnel usually removed them from wounds because the wiggling larvae looked revolting and their movement itched. However, Confederate doctors noticed that maggots helped patients recover from gangrene and other infections because they ate infected flesh but not healthy tissue. Confederate surgeon J.F. Zacharias claimed that "maggots in a single day would clean a wound much better than any other agents we had at our command. I am sure I saved many lives by the use."[119]

PIONEER NEUROLOGISTS

Drugs have long since replaced maggots to heal infections, but some wartime research led to medical theories that are still used today. For example, Union surgeon Silas Weir Mitchell and fellow surgeons Keen and George Morehouse treated soldiers with nerve injuries at Turner's Lane Hospital in Philadelphia. The research Mitchell directed helped establish some of the theories that became the basis for neurology, the study of the human body's nervous system.

Mitchell, Keen, and Morehouse were intrigued by how damaged nerves had created symptoms in patients that seemed to have no physical basis. For example, many soldiers experienced terrible pain long after their wounds had healed physically. Mitchell theorized that this pain was from nerve damage and named it "causalgia." He claimed this intense, nonstop pain was different than pain from a physical wound. He said that it was so powerful that "under such torments the temper changes, the most amiable grow irritable, the soldier becomes a coward, and the strongest man is scarcely less nervous than the most hysterical girl."[120]

One of the most mystifying nerve symptoms was the continuing pain soldiers felt in arms and legs that had been amputated, a sensation that became known as "phantom pain." Mitchell, who treated many soldiers with such pain, theorized that the pain came from nerve endings in the brain that had received signals in the past from the amputated limb and were deceived into thinking the limb was still present. He wrote extensively on the subject, including a short story, "The Case of George Dedlow," in which a soldier with multiple amputations vividly describes what such pain feels like.

Turner's Lane was the first hospital devoted to nerve disorders. There, Mitchell, Keen, and Morehouse researched how nerve injuries from gunshot and other wounds caused unusual or disabling physical symptoms such as paralysis, epileptic seizures, and muscular contractions that were rarely seen by other doctors. In 1864 they coauthored *Gunshot Wounds and Other Injuries of Nerves*, which featured the first descriptions of disorders such as phantom pain and causalgia and quickly became the standard reference book on nerve injuries.

Mitchell, whose work on nerve injury was so influential that he is considered the father of neurology, was as excited about helping soldiers as about doing research. In an 1864 letter to his sister, Mitchell wrote, "It is such a pleasure to see men who have drifted hopeless and helpless from Hospital to Hospital with dead limbs or moveless below the waist to see them walking about and grateful even to tears. I have just cured a charming old naval captain of paralysis from wounds. You never saw a man so pleased."[121]

The only effective treatment the three doctors found to ease nerve pain was morphine, a refined form of opium, and they gave their patients more than forty thousand injections of this drug. However, they were not the only physicians who used narcotic drugs to help their patients.

DRUG ADDICTION

For Civil War doctors, opium and morphine were two of their most dependable drugs. Doctors gave soldiers chunks of raw opium to stop diarrhea, and they prescribed opium pills and powder for pain relief. Morphine, a painkiller, came in the form of a pill or powder, which doctors sprinkled directly on wounds. The powder could also be put into a solution and injected with a hypodermic syringe, a new medical device that became popular during the war.

Unfortunately, Civil War doctors did not realize that soldiers could become addicted to opium and morphine. So many Union and Confederate veterans became hooked on these powerful drugs that after the war such addiction became known as soldier's disease or army disease. In 1879 Union surgeon Joseph Janvier Woodward expressed his concern about using opium and morphine so freely to treat medical problems: "I confess, the more I learn of the behavior of such cases under treatment, the more I am inclined to advise that opiates should be as far as possible avoided."[122]

In this period opium was freely available to soldiers and civilians, who could buy it in many forms. One of the most common ways people took this drug was in laudanum, a mixture of opium and alcohol that people drank to relax their nerves, sleep, or to ease pain. The ease in obtaining opium in the postwar era allowed many soldiers to continue the addictions they acquired from army medical care.

❧ GEORGE DEDLOW'S PHANTOM PAIN ☙

Union surgeon Silas Weir Mitchell did some of the first important research on phantom pain, the sensations people continue to have in arms and legs that have been amputated. His writing on this subject includes "The Case of George Dedlow," a short story that appeared in 1866 in Atlantic Monthly *magazine about a Union surgeon who had both of his legs and one arm amputated. Upon waking from the final surgery, Dedlow felt he was "now a useless torso, more like some strange larval creature than anything of human shape. Of my anguish and horror of myself I dare not speak." In this selection from the story, as printed on the University of Virginia Library's Electronic Text Internet site, Dedlow claimed he could feel his legs after they had been amputated.*

I awoke to consciousness in a hospital-tent. I got hold of my own identity in a moment or two, and was suddenly aware of a sharp cramp in my left leg. I tried to get at it to rub it with my single arm, but, finding myself too weak, hailed an attendant.

Amputations often left patients feeling ghost pains in the areas where missing limbs had been severed.

"Just rub my left calf," said I, "if you please."

"Calf?" said he. "You ain't none. It's took off."

"I know better," said I. "I have pain in both legs."

"Wall, I never!" said he. "You ain't got nary leg."

As I did not believe him, he threw off the covers, and, to my horror, showed me that I had suffered amputation of both thighs, very high up.

"That will do," said I, faintly.

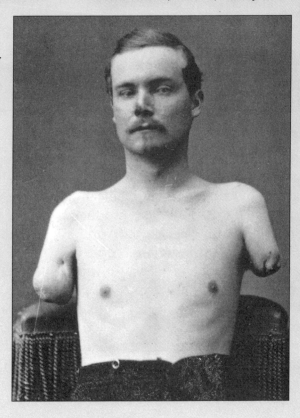

ᴄᴊ CIVIL WAR "NOSTALGIA" ᴋᴏ

Although Civil War doctors knew little about mental illness, they recognized one mental condition as a disease—"nostalgia." The name referred to the overwhelming sadness soldiers felt because they were far from home. More than fifty-five hundred Union soldiers were treated for nostalgia, and seventy-four actually died from this powerful homesickness. Prisoners of war were especially vulnerable to nostalgia. The following description of a Union soldier who died while held by the Confederates is from an article on combat mental health problems from a U.S. Army Internet site. The Confederate report notes that the soldier's physical symptoms were similar to the symptoms experienced by other soldiers suffering from nostalgia.

He would sit for hours with his face in his hands and elbows on his knees, gazing out upon the mass of men and huts with vacant lack-luster eyes. We could not interest him in anything. We tried to show him how to fix his blanket up to give him some shelter, but he went back to work in a disheartened way and finally smiled feebly and stopped. His mind seemed to be fixed on his wife and children. When he first arrived, he ate his rations but finally began to reject them. In a short time he was delirious with hunger and homesickness. He would sit in the sand for hours, imagining that he was at the family table, dispensing his frugal hospitalities to his wife and children. In a short time he died.

THE GREATEST ACHIEVEMENT

Although the use of opiates was not a worthwhile, long-term medical innovation, the Civil War produced many that would benefit the world in the future. Many historians believe the most significant was the way in which medical care was delivered to wounded soldiers. This was accomplished by improving methods to evacuate wounded soldiers from the battlefield and by creating different types of medical facilities in which they could be treated.

The system Union surgeon Jonathan Letterman established to perform those vital tasks provided the basis for handling wounded U.S. soldiers for over a century. The importance of Letterman's plan can be seen in a remark made by Major General Paul Hawley, one of America's top medical officers in the 1940s: "There was not a day during World War II that I did not thank God for Jonathan Letterman."[123]

CONCLUSION

CIVIL WAR DOCTORS CRITIQUE THEMSELVES

The medical battles Union and Confederate doctors waged to save the lives of sick and wounded soldiers were as difficult, demanding, and sometimes dangerous as the armed clashes that made the Civil War the most terrible conflict in the nation's history. In an 1889 speech, Confederate surgeon F. Peyre Porcher praised doctors for the difficulties they endured to do their jobs:

> We are now entitled to award them the highest credit for the unselfish performance of duty— whether done within the walls of a hospital, to the sick or wounded soldier in his quarters, or, as was often the case, in the face of the enemy, surrounded by danger and death. Half starved, upon the coarsest food, in cold and storm and rain, exposed to every hazard—these, our brethren of the medical department, quailed not; they patiently submitted to every hardship, often with systems shattered by privation and ill-health, whilst they performed services which required skill, care and serene courage.[124]

Porcher's lavish praise was warranted. Doctors on both sides risked their lives and endured much physically and emotionally to provide the best medical care they could to millions of soldiers. Yet in the decades following the conflict, many doctors were much harsher in assessing their performance. One of them was Union surgeon John S. Billings, who stated critically in a 1905 address, "Looking back at the war as I remember it, it is a wonder that so many of the medical officers did as well as they did, and that the results were as good as they were."[125]

In their own way, Porcher and Billings were both correct in their assessments of the work done by Civil War doctors. The difference lies in the perspective that each took in making that judgment.

A DIFFICULT JOB

Porcher and many others since him have praised Civil War doctors because they understood how difficult it was for those physicians to care for so many sick and wounded soldiers. Overall, Union and Confederate physicians treated about 10 million cases of injury and illness. Confederate surgeon Herbert M. Nash said that because a typical Southern soldier was disabled six times by wounds or sickness during the course of the war, it was a miracle doctors were able to keep them healthy enough to continue fighting. Nash attested, "Such records demonstrate beyond dispute the grand triumphs and glory of medicine, proving the physician [was] the preserver and defender of armies during war."[126]

The job Civil War doctors did was also made difficult by the conditions under which they worked. They faced danger from fighting that continued around them, they worked in drafty barns or shady spots under trees, and they constantly battled shortages of medical supplies. Those factors all made it harder for doctors to treat patients. Confederate assistant surgeon William H. Taylor once claimed, "I find that [my experience] may be summed up in the statement that I gained an excellent working knowledge of the art of practicing medicine without medicines and surgery without surgical appliances [instruments]."[127]

Despite such obstacles, Union surgeon Silas Weir Mitchell said doctors not only saved the lives of tens of thousands of soldiers but also made important contributions to military medical care and medical knowledge. Mitchell also believed doctors did all that without ever being truly appreciated for their great accomplishments. Mitchell stated, "We had served faithfully as great a cause as earth has known; we built novel hospitals, organized an ambulance service as had never before been seen, contributed numberless essays on disease and wounds, and passed again into private life the unremembered, unrewarded servants of duty."[128]

Civil War doctors believed they deserved praise for working hard to save the lives of so many soldiers. But as the decades went by, many of them began to be critical of the primitive medical knowledge they had carried into battle.

FATAL IGNORANCE

The great medical tragedy of the Civil War is that it was fought shortly before scientific breakthroughs were made that could have saved the lives of tens of thousands of soldiers. It was only a few years after the war ended that new theories about bacteria and infection were discovered by European scientists Louis Pasteur and James Lister. Pasteur proved bacteria caused infection, and Lister discovered he could prevent wound infections by using antiseptic agents such as carbolic acid to kill bacteria.

That knowledge would have helped Civil War doctors greatly reduce the number of deaths from wound infections, many of which they caused themselves by operating in filthy conditions that bred bacteria. In the next few decades after the war, researchers also discovered how bacteria and viruses caused many diseases. That knowledge would have helped Civil War doctors curb diseases such as typhoid fever, which killed thousands of soldiers.

Most historians say Civil War doctors cannot be blamed for the way they cared for soldiers because they simply did not know any better. Many doctors who lived to see those breakthroughs, however, were very upset that their medical ignorance had cost thousands of soldiers their lives. Union surgeon W.W. Keen lamented

this when he wrote, "In the Civil War we knew absolutely nothing of 'germs.' [The knowledge of what causes disease]—the youngest and greatest science to aid in the conquest of death—did not exist."[129] Confederate surgeon Herbert M. Nash was even more blunt in discussing what might have been. He claimed that if doctors had known those theories, then "many brave men of both armies might have been saved to their country!"[130]

A LASTING LESSON

The fact that doctors did not have such knowledge was an unavoidable tragedy. However, even if they had known how to fight infection and disease, hundreds of thousands of soldiers still would have died in the war's terrible fighting. And no group knew the terrible human cost of war better than the doctors who had to heal bodies ripped apart by combat or worn down by disease. Keen claimed that the most important lesson doctors learned was how terrible war is. Keen concluded, "Those of us who went through the Civil War are the most anxious to avoid another war. Only a righteous and noble cause can justify such sacrifices and suffering."[131]

NOTES

INTRODUCTION: WHY DOCTORS WENT TO WAR

1. Quoted in Rebecca Walker, "A Missouri Civil War Surgeon's Letters," Missouri in the Civil War. www.rootsweb.com/~mo civwar/WalkerLetter.html.
2. Quoted in Documenting the American South, *The Autobiography of Joseph Le Conte.* http://docsouth.unc.edu/leconte/lecon te.html.
3. Quoted in Holland Thompson, ed., *The Photographic History of the Civil War,* vol. 7, *Prisons and Hospitals.* Secaucus, NJ: Blue & Grey, 1987, p. 220.
4. Quoted in Alfred Jay Bollet, *Civil War Medicine: Challenges and Triumphs.* Tucson: Galen, 2002, p. 83.

CHAPTER 1: A WAR FOR WHICH DOCTORS WERE ILL-PREPARED

5. Quoted in Albert Castel, ed., "On the Duties of the Surgeon in Action: Surgeon Richard Vickery Provides a Vivid First-hand Glimpse at the Agony That Came with Every Battle," *Civil War Times Illustrated,* June 1978, p. 15.
6. Quoted in Jim Janke, "Dr. David Warman: Contract Surgeon," July 16, 2002. www.homepages. dsu.edu/jankej/civilwar/ warman.html.
7. Quoted in H.H. Cunningham, *Doctors in Gray: The Confederate Medical Service.* Baton Rouge: Louisiana State University Press, 1958, p. 32.
8. Quoted in Thompson, *The Photographic History of the Civil War,* p. 225.
9. Quoted in Cunningham, *Doctors in Gray,* p. 35.
10. Quoted in University of Toledo Libraries, "Medicine in the Civil War." www.cl.utoledo.edu/cana day/quackery/quack8.html.
11. Quoted in Paul E. Steiner, *Disease in the Civil War: Natural Biological Warfare in 1861–1865.* Springfield, II: Charles C. Thomas, 1968, p. 220.
12. William H. Taylor, "Some Experiences of a Confederate Assistant Surgeon," Society of Civil War Surgeons. www.civil warsurgeons.org/articles/experi ence.htm.
13. Herbert M. Nash, "Some Reminiscences of a Confederate Surgeon," Society of Civil War Surgeons. www.civilwarsurgeons. org/articles/reminiscences%20 nash.htm.

14. Taylor, "Some Experiences of a Confederate Assistant Surgeon."
15. Simon Baruch, "Experiences as a Confederate Surgeon," *Civil War Times Illustrated*, October 1965, p. 41.
16. Quoted in Walker, "A Missouri Civil War Surgeon's Letters."
17. Quoted in Robert E. Denney, *Civil War Medicine: Care & Comfort of the Wounded*. New York: Sterling, 1994, p. 35.
18. Quoted in Denney. *Civil War Medicine*, p. 8.
19. Quoted in Janke, "Dr. David Warman."
20. Quoted in Bollet, *Civil War Medicine*, p. 128.
21. Quoted in Denney, *Civil War Medicine*, p. 93.
22. Quoted in Guy R. Hasegawa, "The Civil War's Medical Cadets: Medical Students Serving the Union," *Journal of the American College of Surgeons*, July 2001, p. 88.
23. Hunter Holmes McGuire, "Dr. McGuire's Address on Progress of Medicine in the South, 1889," Civil War Talk. www.civilwar talk.com/cwt_alt/resources /medicine/primary/medsconfed. htm.

CHAPTER 2: TREATING SOLDIERS WOUNDED IN BATTLE
24. Quoted in Denney, *Civil War Medicine*, p. 161.
25. Quoted in Frank R. Freemon,

Gangrene and Glory: Medical Care During the American Civil War. Cranbury, NJ: Associated University Presses, 1998, p. 76.
26. Jonathan A. Letterman, "Dr. Letterman's Report on Antietam," Civil War Talk. www.civilwartalk. com/cwt_alt/resources/medicine /primary/antietam.htm.
27. Quoted in "Dr. Letterman's Gettysburg Report," Civil War Talk. www.civilwartalk/cw_alt/ resources/medicine/primary/ gettysburg.htm.
28. John S. Billings, "Medical Reminiscenses of the Civil War," Society of Civil War Surgeons. www.civilwarsurgeons.org/ articles/medical%20reminis cences.htm.
29. Taylor, "Some Experiences of a Confederate Assistant Surgeon."
30. W.W. Keen, "Surgical Reminiscences of the Civil War," Society of Civil War Surgeons. www. civilwarsurgeons.org/articles/sur gical%20reminiscences.htm.
31. Quoted in Denney, *Civil War Medicine*, p. 34.
32. Quoted in Bell Irvin Wiley, *The Life of Billy Yank: The Common Soldier of the Union*. Baton Rouge: Louisiana State University Press, 1971, p. 265.
33. Quoted in Virginia Tech University Libraries Special Collections Department, "Memoir of Archibald Atkinson, Jr.," October

17, 1996. http://spec.lib.vt.edu/civwar/memoirs.htm.

34. Quoted in Denney, *Civil War Medicine*, p. 197.

35. Quoted in Thompson, *The Photographic History of the Civil War*, p. 262.

36. Quoted in Walker, "A Missouri Civil War Surgeon's Letters."

37. Hunter McGuire, "Death of Stonewall Jackson." www.members.aol.com/CWSurgeon0/jdeth.html.

38. Quoted in Rutherford B. Hayes Presidential Center, "Dr. John B. Rice, Civil War Surgeon," December 2002. www.rbhayes.org/papertrail/jb_rice.html.

39. Quoted in Janet King, "Civil War Medicine," Vermont in the Civil War, 2004. www.vermontcivilwar.org/medic/medicine 4.shtml.

40. Quoted in Thompson, *The Photographic History of the Civil War*, p. 264.

41. Letterman, "Dr. Letterman's Report on Antietam."

42. Quoted in Alfred Jay Bollet, "The Truth About Civil War Surgery," *Civil War Times*, October 2004, p. 22.

43. Quoted in Bollet, *Civil War Medicine*, p. 124.

CHAPTER 3: DOCTORS ON THE BATTLEFIELD

44. Quoted in Virginia Tech University Libraries Special Collections Department, "Isaac White Letters, 1861–1938." http://spec.lib.vt.edu/mss/white/white.htm.

45. Letterman, "Dr. Letterman's Gettysburg Report."

46. McGuire, "Dr. McGuire's Address on Progress of Medicine in the South."

47. Quoted in Harold Elk Straubing, *In Hospital and Camp: The Civil War Through the Eyes of Its Doctors and Nurses*. Harrisburg, PA: Stackpole, 1963, p. 15.

48. Alfred Lewis Castleman, *The Army of the Potomac: Behind the Scenes*. Milwaukee: Strickland, 1863, p. 230.

49. Quoted in Walker, "A Missouri Civil War Surgeon's Letters."

50. Quoted in Hasegawa, "The Civil War's Medical Cadets."

51. Quoted in Virginia Tech University Libraries Special Collections Department, "Isaac White Letters, 1861–1938."

52. Castleman, *The Army of the Potomac*, p. 45.

53. Baruch, "Experiences as a Confederate Surgeon," p. 46.

54. Taylor, "Some Experiences of a Confederate Assistant Surgeon."

55. Quoted in Straubing, *In Hospital and Camp*, p. 63.

56. Nash, "Some Reminiscences of a Confederate Surgeon."

57. Quoted in Janke, "Dr. David Warman."

58. Quoted in Denney, *Civil War Medicine*, p. 307.

59. Taylor, "Some Experiences of a Confederate Assistant Surgeon."

60. Keen, "Surgical Reminiscences of the Civil War."

61. Quoted in Castel, "On the Duties of the Surgeon in Action."

62. Quoted in Bollet, *Civil War Medicine*, p. 122.

63. Quoted in Denney, *Civil War Medicine*, p. 103.

64. Quoted in Straubing, *In Hospital and Camp*, p. 17.

65. Quoted in Virginia Military Institute Archives, "Napoleon B. Brisbine Letters," www.vmi.edu/archives /Manuscripts/ms0391.html.

66. Quoted in Allen Mikaelian, *Medal of Honor: Profiles of America's Military Heroes from the Civil War to the Present*. New York: Hyperion, 2002, p. 9.

67. Baruch, "Experiences as a Confederate Surgeon," p. 42.

Chapter 4: Staffing Civil War Hospitals

68. Quoted in Cunningham, *Doctors in Gray*, p. 46.

69. Quoted in Bollet, *Civil War Medicine*, p. 217.

70. Castleman, *The Army of the Potomac*, p. 63.

71. Quoted in Virginia Tech University Libraries Special Collections Department, "Memoir of Archibald Atkinson, Jr."

72. Keen, "Surgical Reminiscences of the Civil War."

73. Keen, "Surgical Reminiscences of the Civil War."

74. Thompson, *The Photographic History of the Civil War*, p. 262.

75. Quoted in Cunningham, *Doctors in Gray*, p. 56.

76. Quoted in Cunningham, *Doctors in Gray*, p. 63.

77. Quoted in Walker, "A Missouri Civil War Surgeon's Letters."

78. Quoted in Janke, "Dr. David Warman."

79. Quoted in Fort Delaware, "Washington Nugent—Union Surgeon." www.visitthefort.com /nugent.html.

80. Quoted in Gerald Schwartz, ed., *A Woman Doctor's Civil War: Esther Hill Hawks' Diary*. Columbia: University of South Carolina Press, 1984, p. 51.

81. Quoted in Janke, "Dr. David Warman."

82. Quoted in Cunningham, *Doctors in Gray*, p. 72.

83. Castleman, *The Army of the Potomac*, p. 87.

84. Walt Whitman, *Memoranda During the War*. Bloomington: Indiana University Press, 1962, p. 18.

85. Whitman, *Memoranda During the War*, p. 22.

86. Quoted in Denney, *Civil War Medicine*, p. 109.

CHAPTER 5: FIGHTING DISEASE, THE CIVIL WAR'S PRIME KILLER

87. Quoted in Peter Josyph, ed., *The Wounded River: The Civil War Letters of John Vance Lauderdale, M.D.* East Lansing: Michigan State University Press, 1993, p. 57.
88. Quoted in Virginia Tech University Libraries Special Collections Department, "Memoir of Archibald Atkinson, Jr."
89. Quoted in Cunningham, *Doctors in Gray*, p. 195.
90. Quoted in Denney, *Civil War Medicine*, p. 85.
91. U.S. Sanitary Commission, "Sanitary Commission No. 17." www.netwalk.com/~jpr/17.html.
92. Quoted in Bell Irvin Wiley, *They Who Fought Here.* New York: Macmillan, 1959, p. 215.
93. Quoted in Michigan Historical Center, "A Michigan Civil War Physician's Diary," www.michigan.gov/hal/0,1607,7_160_17451-18670-18793_52963_,00.html.
94. Quoted in Thompson, *The Photographic History of the Civil War*, p. 236.
95. Keen, "Surgical Reminiscences of the Civil War."
96. Quoted in Bollet, *Civil War Medicine*, p. 203.
97. Quoted in Michigan Historical Center, "A Michigan Civil War Physician's Diary."
98. Edward Warren, *An Epitome of Practical Surgery for Field and Hospital*, Documenting the American South, http://docsouth.unc.edu/imls/warrene/warrene.html.
99. Quoted in Otto Eisenschiml, "Medicine in the War," *Civil War Times Illustrated*, May 1962, p. 6.
100. Nash, "Some Reminiscences of a Confederate Surgeon."
101. Quoted in Bollet, *Civil War Medicine*, p. 293.
102. Castleman, *The Army of the Potomac*, p. 7.
103. Castleman, *The Army of the Potomac*, p. 60.
104. Quoted in Cunningham, *Doctors in Gray*, p. 206.
105. Billings, "Medical Reminiscences of the Civil War."
106. Quoted in Gerald W. Ritter, "Civil War Letters of John Alexander Ritter, M.D., 49th Indiana Volunteers." http://gwillritter.tripod.com/jarlettersl.htm.
107. Quoted in Ritter, "Civil War Letters of John Alexander Ritter, M.D., 49th Indiana Volunteers."
108. Quoted in Janke, "Dr. David Warman."

CHAPTER 6: CIVIL WAR INNOVATIONS IN MEDICAL CARE

109. Quoted in National Museum of Health and Medicine, "A Brief

History of the Collecting of Anatomical Specimens by the Army Medical Museum." www.nmhm.washingtondc.museum/collections/anatomical/articles/brief_history.html.

110. McGuire, "Death of Stonewall Jackson."

111. Quoted in Mary C. Gillett, *The Army Medical Department, 1818–1865*. Washington, DC: U.S. Army Center for Military History, 1987, p. 220.

112. Keen, "Surgical Reminiscences of the Civil War."

113. Quoted in Freemon, *Gangrene and Glory*, p. 182.

114. Quoted in National Museum of Health and Medicine, "Abraham Lincoln: The Final Casualty of the War." www.nmhm.washingtondc.museum/exhibits/nationswounds/lincoln.html.

115. McGuire, "Dr. McGuire's Address on Progress of Medicine in the South."

116. Quoted in Bollet, *Civil War Medicine*, p. 177.

117. Quoted in Colin F. Baxter, "Dr. James Baxter Bean, Civil War Dentist," *Journal of East Tennessee History*, 1995, p. 42.

118. Keen, "Surgical Reminiscences of the Civil War."

119. Quoted in Riverdeep Interactive Learning Center, "Bug Medicine: War Stories," March 4, 2002. www.riverdeep.net/current/2002/03/030402_bug medicine.jhtml.

120. Quoted in David Berg, "Silas Weir Mitchell: Nerve Pain Pioneer," PainOnline, 2001. www.painonline.org/mitchell.htm.

121. Quoted in Nancy Cervetti, "S. Weir Mitchell: The Early Years," *American Pain Society Bulletin*, March 2003. www.am-painsoc.org/pub/bulletin/mar03/histl. htm.

122. Quoted in Richard Severo and Lewis Milford, *The Wages of War: When America's Soldiers Came Home from Valley Forge to Vietnam*. New York: Simon and Schuster, 1990, p. 227.

123. Quoted in Bollet, *Civil War Medicine*, p. 293.

Conclusion: Civil War Doctors Critique Themselves

124. F. Peyre Porcher, "An Account of the Confederate Surgeon," eHistory, www.ehistory.com/uscw/features/medicine/cwsurgeon/csasurgeons.cfm.

125. Billings, "Medical Reminiscences of the Civil War."

126. Nash, "Some Reminiscences of a Confederate Surgeon."

127. Taylor, "Some Experiences of a Confederate Assistant Surgeon."

128. Quoted in Bollet, *Civil War Medicine*, p. 444.

129. Quoted in Wiley, *The Life of Billy Yank,* p. 125.

130. Nash, "Some Reminiscences of a Confederate Surgeon."

131. Keen, "Surgical Reminiscences of the Civil War."

FOR FURTHER READING

Robert E. Denney, *Civil War Medicine: Care & Comfort of the Wounded*. New York: Sterling, 1994. Excerpts from diaries, battle reports, and other sources arranged in a daily chronology provide an interesting look at how doctors worked.

Frank R. Freemon, *Gangrene and Glory: Medical Care During the American Civil War*. Cranbury, NJ: Associated University Presses, 1998. A basic guide to how doctors treated injuries and illnesses.

Francis A. Lord, *They Fought for the Union*. Harrisburg, PA: Stackpole, 1960. An easy-to-read book about doctors and other Civil War soldiers.

Gerald Schwartz, ed., *A Woman Doctor's Civil War: Esther Hill Hawks' Diary*. Columbia: University of South Carolina Press, 1984. The diary of one of only two female doctors in the Civil War.

Harold Elk Straubing, *In Hospital and Camp: The Civil War Through the Eyes of Its Doctors and Nurses*. Harrisburg, PA: Stackpole, 1963. This book contains first-person narratives by several doctors and nurses.

Bell Irvin Wiley, *They Who Fought Here*. New York: Macmillan, 1959. A general introduction to the Civil War, including material on medical care.

WORKS CONSULTED

BOOKS

Alfred Jay Bollet, *Civil War Medicine: Challenges and Triumphs*. Tucson: Galen, 2002. In one of the best books on Civil War doctors, the author evaluates the work they did from a medical standpoint.

Alfred Lewis Castleman, *The Army of the Potomac: Behind the Scenes*. Milwaukee: Strickland, 1863. A memoir by the surgeon for the Fifth Wisconsin Volunteers.

H.H. Cunningham, *Doctors in Gray: The Confederate Medical Service*. Baton Rouge: Louisiana State University Press, 1958. The most comprehensive history written about Confederate doctors.

Mary C. Gillett, *The Army Medical Department, 1818–1865*. Washington, DC. U.S. Army Center for Military History, 1987. A detailed history of Union medical care in this period.

Peter Josyph, ed., *The Wounded River: The Civil War Letters of John Vance Lauderdale, M.D.* East Lansing: Michigan State University Press, 1993. An interesting look at one doctor's experience in the Civil War.

Allen Mikaelian, *Medal of Honor: Profiles of America's Military Heroes from the Civil War to the Present*. New York: Hyperion, 2002. This book includes a biography of Mary Walker, a Union surgeon.

Richard Severo and Lewis Milford, *The Wages of War: When America's Soldiers Came Home from Valley Forge to Vietnam*. New York: Simon and Schuster, 1990. This anthology includes a section on what happened to Civil War veterans.

Paul E. Steiner, *Disease in the Civil War: Natural Biological Warfare in 1861–1865*. Springfield, IL: Charles C. Thomas, 1968. A scientific look at the war's diseases.

Holland Thompson, ed., *The Photographic History of the Civil War*. Vol. 7. *Prisons and Hospitals*. Secaucus, NJ: Blue & Grey, 1987. Union and Confederate surgeons wrote the articles in the section on medical care.

Walt Whitman, *Memoranda During the War*. Bloomington: Indiana University Press, 1962. In this reprint of his 1863 book, Whitman describes his experiences in Union hospitals.

Bell Irvin Wiley, *The Life of Billy Yank: The Common Soldier of the Union*. Baton Rouge: Louisiana State

University Press, 1971. An interesting, well-documented study of daily life for soldiers, including their medical care.

PERIODICALS
Simon Baruch, "Experiences as a Confederate Surgeon," *Civil War Times Illustrated*, October 1965.

Colin F. Baxter, "Dr. James Baxter Bean, Civil War Dentist" *Journal of East Tennessee History*, 1995.

Alfred Jay Bollet, "The Truth About Civil War Surgery," *Civil War Times*, October 2004.

Albert Castel, ed., "On the Duties of the Surgeon in Action: Surgeon Richard Vickery Provides a Vivid First-hand Glimpse at the Agony That Came with Every Battle," *Civil War Times Illustrated*, June 1978.

Otto Eisenschiml, "Medicine in the War," *Civil War Times Illustrated*, May 1962.

Guy R. Hasegawa, "The Civil War's Medical Cadets: Medical Students Serving the Union," *Journal of the American College of Surgeons*, July 2001.

INTERNET SOURCES
David Berg, "Silas Weir Mitchell: Nerve Pain Pioneer," PainOnline, 2001. www.painonline.org/ mitchell.htm.

John S. Billings, "Medical Reminiscences of the Civil War," Society of Civil War Surgeons. www. civilwarsurgeons.org/articles /medical%20reminiscences.htm.

Nancy Cervetti, "S. Weir Mitchell: The Early Years," *American Pain Society Bulletin,* March 2003. www.ampainsoc.org/pub/bul letin/mar03/hist1.htm.

Documenting the American South, *The Autobiography of Joseph Le Conte.* http://docsouth.unc.edu /leconte/leconte.html.

Fort Delaware, "Washington Nugent —Union Surgeon." www.visit thefort.com/nugent.html.

Albert Julius Glass and Franklin D. Jones, "Psychiatry in the U.S. Army: Lessons for Community Psychiatry," Uniformed Services, University of the Health Sciences, Learning Resource Center. www. lrc.usuhs.mil/archivex/pdf/ CombatPsych.pdf.

Joseph Jacobs, "Some of the Drug Conditions During the War Between the States, 1861–5," Home of the American Civil War. www.civilwarhome.com/ drugsshsp.htm.

Jim Janke, "Dr. David Warman: Contract Surgeon," July 16, 2002. www.homepages.dsu.edu/ jankej/civilwar/warman.html.

W.W. Keen, "Surgical Reminiscences of the Civil War," Society of Civil War Surgeons. www.civil

warsurgeons.org/articles/surgi
cal%20reminiscences.htm.

Janet King, "Civil War Medicine,"
Vermont in the Civil War, 2004.
www.vermontcivilwar.org/medic
/medicine4.shtml.

Jonathan A. Letterman, "Dr. Letterman's
Gettysburg Report," Civil War
Talk. www.civilwartalk.com/
cwt_alt/resources/medicine
/primary/gettysburg.htm.

———, "Dr. Letterman's Report on
Antietam," Civil War Talk. www.
civilwartalk.com/cwt_alt/
resources/medicine/primary/
antietam.htm.

Hunter McGuire, "Death of Stonewall
Jackson." www.members.aol.
com/CWSurgeon0/jdeth.html.

Hunter Holmes McGuire, "Dr.
McGuire's Address on Progress
of Medicine in the South," Civil
War Talk. www.civilwartalk.com
/cwt_alt/resources/medi
cine/primary/medsconfed.htm.

Michigan Historical Center, "A
Michigan Civil War Physician's
Diary," www.michigan.gov/
hal/0,1607,7-160-17451_18670_
18793-52963-,00.html.

Herbert M. Nash, "Some Reminiscences of a Confederate Surgeon,"
Society of Civil War Surgeons,
www.civilwarsurgeons. org/arti
cles/reminiscences%20nash
.htm.

National Museum of Health and
Medicine, "Abraham Lincoln:
The Final Casualty of the War."
www.nmhm.washingtondc.mus
eum/exhibits/nationswounds
/lincoln.html.

———, "A Brief History of the
Collecting of Anatomical Specimens
by the Army Medical Museum."
www.nmhm.washingtondc.
museum/collections/anatomical
/articles/brief_history.html.

F. Peyre Porcher, "An Account of the
Confederate Surgeon," eHistory,
www.ehistory.com/uscw/
features/medicine/cwsurgeon
/csasurgeons.cfm.

Gerald W. Ritter, "Civil War Letters
of John Alexander Ritter, M.D.,
49th Indiana Volunteers." http://
gwillritter.tripod.com/jarlet
ters1.htm.

Riverdeep Interactive Learning Center,
"Bug Medicine: War Stories,"
March 4, 2002. www. riverdeep.
net/current/2002/03/030
402_bugmedicine. jhtml.

Rutherford B. Hayes Presidential
Center, "Civil War Soldier
William C. Caldwell," February
2000. www.rbhayes.org/papertrail
/caldwell.html.

———, "Dr. John B. Rice, Civil War
Surgeon," December 2002. www.
rbhayes.org/papertrail/jb_rice.
html.

William H. Taylor, "Some Experiences
of a Confederate Assistant

Surgeon," Society of Civil War Surgeons, www.civilwarsurgeons. org/articles/experience.htm.

University of Toledo Libraries, "Medicine in the Civil War." www.cl.utoledo.edu/canaday /quackery/quack8.html.

University of Virginia Library Electronic Text Center, "The Autobiography of a Quack" and "The Case of George Dedlow," 1999. www.etext.lib.virginia.edu /modeng/modeng0.browse .html.

U.S. Sanitary Commission, "Sanitary Commission No. 17." www.net walk.com/~jpr/17.html.

Virginia Military Institute Archives, "Napoleon B. Brisbine Letters," www.vmi.edu/archives/Manu scripts/ms0391.html.

Virginia Tech University Libraries Special Collections Department, "Isaac White Letters, 1861– 1938." http://spec.lib.vt.edu/ mss/white/white.htm.

———, "Memoir of Archibald Atkinson, Jr.," October 17, 1996. http://spec.lib.vt.edu/civwar/ memoirs.htm.

Rebecca Walker, "A Missouri Civil War Surgeon's Letters," Missouri in the Civil War. www.roots web.com/~mocivwar/Walker Letter.html.

Edward Warren, *An Epitome of Practical Surgery for Field and Hospital*, Documenting the American South, http://doc south.unc.edu/imls/warrene /warrene.html.

WEB SITES

Documenting the American South (http://docsouth.unc.edu). This University of North Carolina Web site includes electronic texts of Civil War documents and books.

eHistory (www.ehistory.com/uscw/ index.cfm). This Web site, which provides information on every period in history, has excellent articles, background information, and first-person narratives on Civil War doctors and medical care.

National Museum of Civil War Medicine (www.civilwarmed. org). The Web site for the museum on Civil War medicine in Fredricksburg, Virginia, is a good source of information on doctors and medical care. It includes photographs, articles, and links to other sites.

National Museum of Health and Medicine (www.nmhm.washington dc.museum). The museum, originally called the Army Medical Museum, was founded in 1862 during the Civil War. The Web site for the museum has many historical photographs and articles on doctors and medicine during the war.

The Society of Civil War Surgeons (www.civilwarsurgeons.org). The society preserves the history of and educates the public on Civil War doctors. The site includes photographs, articles, and first-person narratives from Union and Confederate doctors.

INDEX

ABOUT THE AUTHOR

Michael V. Uschan has written more than forty books, including *The Korean War*, for which he won the 2002 Council of Wisconsin Writers Juvenile Nonfiction Award. Mr. Uschan began his career as a writer and editor with United Press International, a wire service that provides stories to newspapers, radio, and television. Journalism is sometimes called "history in a hurry." Mr. Uschan considers writing history books a natural extension of the skills he developed in his many years as a journalist. He and his wife, Barbara, reside in the Milwaukee suburb of Franklin, Wisconsin.